KINGDOM CONFLICT

JOSEPH M. STOWELL

Triumph in the
Midst of Testing

KINGDOM CONFLICT

MOODY PRESS
CHICAGO

Revised and Expanded Edition © 1996 by
JOSEPH M. STOWELL

Original Edition © 1985 by
SP PUBLICATION
VICTOR BOOKS, WHEATON, ILLINOIS 60187

ISBN: 0-8024-4541-1

1 3 5 7 9 10 8 6 4 2

Printed in the United States of America

To my parents,
Dr. and Mrs. Joseph M. Stowell,
who through many years
helped prepare me
for the conflict

CONTENTS

INTRODUCTION

O nward Christian soldiers, marching as to war."
We all know the old hymn, but to some of us it may be more of a folk song than a battle cry. People used to have a somewhat romantic notion of sending their young men off to war. But today, going to war doesn't have the same connotations that it did when the hymn was written.

These days, some of the most devastating stories you'll ever hear and pictures you'll ever see are from the numerous war zones throughout the world whose locations seem to change from day to day. Buildings demolished. Walls riddled with bullet holes. Shops boarded up. Streets in rubble. And on the faces of those born into such conditions are usually expressions of helplessness and hopelessness.

In a spiritual sense, we too find ourselves born into a major conflict. As soon as we develop any spiritual awareness, we discover we are at war. The difference is that we are not innocent victims. Rather, we are recruits who must choose to fight for one side or the other. We cannot opt to remain neutral in this ongoing battle. It soon becomes *our* battle. The best we can do is know how the conflict started, how we got involved, and what we should do about it. That's what this book is about.

The kingdom conflict, as you will discover, began before the creation of our world. And almost from the moment God created human beings to populate the world, we were drawn into that conflict. We're going to focus on the book of Genesis—more precisely, on the lives of several of the characters in that book. We'll see what we can learn about the kingdom conflict from their successes and failures.

The chapters that follow are a call to arms. You will see the importance of enlisting on the right team, and how to be an effective soldier. You'll be warned of enemy strategies that have worked in the past—strategies you can avoid if you know about them in advance. You'll see the occasional difficulties of showing complete obedience to your Commander in Chief, and the even worse difficulties if you choose not to. Above all, you will see that nothing—absolutely nothing at all—can thwart God's plans or prevent His ultimate victory.

To help you apply what you're learning, you'll find key questions at the end of each chapter. Use these questions as you see fit. Perhaps you can create a group discussion of the material in each chapter. But more important, the questions can be used for self-examination before quickly moving from one chapter to the next. You can read books about battle strategy all day long, but if you never join the battle and put them to use they do you little good.

You will find that just as war can have its devastating consequences, it also has the effect of pulling together those who fight on the same side. Just watch two "war buddies" get together after several years to reminisce about their experiences. With all the stories and laughter, you would hardly know they went through a traumatic experience at all. This is even more evident in the kingdom conflict, because the victories we achieve are eternal ones.

As one of your brothers-in-arms, I want to encourage you to persevere in the conflicts you face on a daily basis. May this book be a comfort and a challenge as you do so.

1

CASUALTIES OF WAR
The Battle Against Alienation from God

My hand froze to the phone. I heard myself say, "Impossible!" When I was a young pastor this man had been a model to me. He had been unusually blessed in the ministry. Now he had left his family and his flock . . . moral failure. I remember thinking, *No one is exempt; I'll never be surprised again.*

Exempt. In a world of loopholes, success often belongs to the clever, the ones who avoid trouble and defeat by exploiting the exemptions: tax exemptions, a bye in the first round of tournament play, a test waived, diplomatic immunity, knowing the right people, being in the right place at the right time. There is, however, a reality from which no one is exempt—the reality of sin. The clever, the spiritual, the young and the old, the affluent and the poor . . . we are all vulnerable to sin's devastating encroachment in our lives.

What else can you conclude when your best friend, the product of a Christian home and uniquely gifted of God, is working on a third marriage? Or when a classmate from college calls from the penitentiary where he is serving time for check forgery? The words blaze their way through my brain: *No one is exempt!*

Sad to say, in recent years public mentality has shifted from shock at the public humiliation and scandal of a "hero" to the cynical attitude of "Who's going to be next?" It seems that each week some shocking revelation about a respected public figure has come to light. No one is excluded—not presidents or preachers, actors or F.B.I. directors, sports figures or Miss Americas.

Recently the director of a well-known national charitable organization was convicted of embezzling $600,000 that had been donated by compassionate contributors. His theft wasn't a matter of desperate personal need. Rather, the money had been used to finance exorbitant vacations for friends and assorted girlfriends. Such stories are distressing enough, but in addition to the incarceration of the guilty person are the consequences to others. The reputation of the whole organization suffers, contributions decline, and many people who could (and should) have been helped will continue to suffer.

Similarly, whenever a "man of God" is caught in a public scandal, his isn't the only reputation that suffers. So does everyone else's who claims to follow the same God—yours and mine included. Even the reputation of a completely holy and righteous God is distorted among the non-Christian world, which watches and judges Christians based on their actions.

The casualties are everywhere. They are the angry, the bitter, the depressed, the apathetic, the fearful, the guilt ridden, the lonely, the victims of broken relationships. They include those who willingly practice sin, thinking that since no one knows, they have beaten the system. The victims are those who are enjoying their sin for a season, refusing to believe that "a man reaps what he sows" (Galatians 6:7). They are those who define success in the accumulation of earthly goods and prestige by their standing in the eyes of men. But they are the conquered ones, the prisoners of war in a supernatural struggle.

We are all vulnerable, all of us. No one is exempt.

THE CONFLICT WITHIN AND WITHOUT

We have all thought at some time, *Satan is attacking my life.* Actually, Satan does not attack us personally. He is not omnipresent and therefore can be only in one place at a time. In fact, God's Word indicates that he spends day and night before the throne of God accusing believers (Revelation 12:10). Even the demonic forces, though there are legions of them, don't normally interact with us personally. They don't need to. Our inner propensity to sin and the network of sin around us are sufficient to ignite the conflict.

The world system, established and crafted by Satan, entices our greed, passion, and pride. It stimulates our fear, anger, and despondency. Satan is the master of this network. God's Word calls it the *cosmos*.

This cosmos, the world around us, appeals to the flesh, the world *within* us. The New Testament consistently labels the sin problem within us as the flesh. Galatians 5 refers to this internal sin problem when it speaks of the conflict between the Spirit and the flesh that goes on in each of us. It then lists the tragic results that come from yielding to the "flesh" within (Galatians 5:16–21).

First John 2:15–16 states, "Do not love the world or anything in the world. If anyone loves the world, the love of the Father is not in him. For everything in the world—the cravings of sinful man, the lust of his eyes and the boasting of what he has and does—comes not from the Father but from the world." Note that "the world" is defined by the stuff within us. Even the hermits who fled to the wilderness in the fourth century, escaping the "world" to become monks, must have soon realized that they took a chunk of the world with them.

Which of us does not feel the inner tug and the craving of sin? Have you never sensed the pull of greed? Who is not stimulated by the lust for what we see? Are there any of us who are exempt from being motivated by the internal spirit of pride in what we have or who we are?

When the "cosmos" within is triggered by the "cosmos" without, we are drawn into the struggle. It's an opportunity to satisfy ourselves at the Spirit's expense. It's a temptation to fantasize about what a great lover someone else would be, to promote ourselves by tearing down another, or to commit any number of offenses that we know and believe to be wrong.

When we yield—when we choose to cultivate the lust of the flesh, the lust of the eyes, and the pride of life—that is when Satan's system capitalizes and we become casualties to his credit.

To be victorious, we must first know ourselves. We must know that our vulnerability often lies in our quickness to excuse a sin. We weaken ourselves by lacking the integrity to admit personal responsibility for our choices. Some of us are conquered simply because we refuse to believe that there is consequence to sin. Take a close look and see if there aren't some kinks in your personal armor.

EXCUSES IN THE CONFLICT

The excuses for sin are a dime a dozen:

- I can't help myself.
- I've always been this way.
- I've tried to change, but I can't.
- I'm better than a lot of other people I know.
- It doesn't hurt anyone, does it?
- It's my environment; it overwhelms me!
- It's the only pleasure I allow myself.

And so the habits of sin and the little "slips" of life are excused. It's really "no big thing."

Excuses are an anesthetic of Satan. They numb us to the operation of sin in our lives. They make us insensitive to sin's impact and deceive us as to our responsibilities. A plumber left a note on his illegally parked car which said, *Plumber at work inside.* Next to the note was a ticket with another note that read, *Cop at work outside.* Like the plumber, we may excuse ourselves and feel quite safe. Yet, in reality we are guilty before God and in jeopardy with Him, eligible for all the consequences of sin.

One of the most satisfying ways of excusing ourselves is to pass the blame. It starts early in life. Johnny comes running in from the backyard, crying and showing teeth marks on his arm, saying, "Daddy, Sally bit me!" Dad wisely responds, "Johnny, why did she bite you? What did you do to her?" "But Daddy, she bit me," he pleads with great urgency. "Yes, but what did *you* do?" After several more tries, seeing that Dad will not be fooled by his attempt to dodge responsibility, Johnny sheepishly confesses, "I punched her in the nose."

The proclivity to blame others for our own wrongful actions began as soon as sin came into the world. When God confronted Adam about his sin, Adam immediately passed the blame on to someone else. You may find this hard to believe, but Adam blamed his wife! He said to God, "The woman . . ." (Genesis 3:12).

But Adam didn't stop there. It is important to note that he ultimately passed the blame to God. He said, "The woman *you put here*" (v. 12, italics added). How often God catches the blame for our sins! We excuse our bitterness and anger by shaking our fists at God for something that He allowed. Perhaps it's the parents God gave us or the bad health that He permitted; or even the "nice" Christian He led you to marry; or the fact that He hasn't answered your prayers or that you are not yet married. It's the job to which He took you or the church He called you to pastor. It may even be the face that God gave you or how short or tall He created you. Excusing ourselves by blaming God as we wallow in our sin reminds me of Job's wife, who advised Job to "curse God and die" (Job 2:9). But Job replied with strength, "Though he slay me, yet will I hope in him" (13:15).

It is foolish to blame God whenever something doesn't work out exactly as we would like it to. We must realize that while God may allow a crisis to impact our lives, He also promises to provide both grace to cope victoriously (2 Corinthians 12:9) and a way to escape that we may be able to bear it (1 Corinthians 10:13).

If you read the rest of Genesis 3, you will see that God is the only One not judged; He was not to blame. Blaming God instead of unconditionally worshiping Him as Lord guarantees continuing heartache and failure.

God then turned to Eve. She too found an excuse for her sin—Satan. "Then the Lord God said to the woman, 'What is this you have done?' The woman said, 'The serpent deceived me, and I ate'" (Genesis 3:13).

Satan frequently gets more credit than he deserves. In literature and media he is often pictured as whispering into a person's ear and controlling every move the person makes. But Scripture makes it clear that he can't conquer us against our will. The truth of the matter is that a believer's new life in Christ guarantees a greater power within us than the power of Satan. John confidently wrote, "The one who is in you is greater than the one who is in the world" (1 John 4:4).

Jesus' resurrection proved the strength of God over all of sin, death, and hell. We are not pawns on the chessboard of the struggle between good and evil; we are not captivated unwillingly by Satan's schemes. Yes, there is a conflict between the kingdom of God and the kingdom of "the prince of this world" (John 12:31). Yet the triumph of God is sure and its potential dwells within us as His loyal followers. It is within us that the issue of triumph or tragedy is settled.

INTEGRITY IN THE CONFLICT

Triumph in this supernatural struggle begins by having enough integrity to dismiss all excuses and take responsibility for what we do. God holds us personally accountable for our attitudes, actions, and responses to life. But accepting this responsibility is a struggle in itself.

I have a friend who fights this tendency constantly. We often joke about how nice it must be to live a guiltless life since everyone else is at fault. Yet whenever we tend to blame our failures on others and our environment, let's remember that Adam and Eve rebelled against God in the perfect environment of the Garden of Eden.

Dumping guilt on others is not the way to achieve a clear conscience. We may not be responsible for all the circumstances we face, but we *are* accountable for our responses in those situations. When we're going through a crisis, we must determine that at the end of it all we will have the inner peace of a clear conscience regardless of the outcome of the situation or the behavior of others. This is the integrity of accepting personal responsibility.

In one Nazi concentration camp a famous German theologian was stripped and brought naked before the commander. In the midst of his humiliation he looked at his accuser and said, "You can take my dignity, wealth, clothes, and family from me. But the one thing you can never take from me is my freedom to respond to you in the way that I choose."

Paul reminded us of this responsibility when he wrote, "For we will all stand before God's judgment seat. It is written: '"As surely as I live," says the Lord, "every knee will bow before me; every tongue will confess to God."' So then, each of us will give an account of *himself* to God" (Romans 14:10–12, italics added).

TAKE IT PERSONALLY

We often preface a conversation by saying, "Don't take this personally." But when it comes to the treachery of sin, we *must* take it personally because sin begins within us! It is an intimate reality.

Just as we genetically reflect our physical parentage, so we reflect a spiritual parentage from Adam in the reality of the sin problem (Romans 5). This internal struggle of the flesh is always with us. We cannot excuse ourselves by blaming sin on external factors. This becomes clear as James details for us the pattern of sin. "When tempted, no one should say, 'God is tempting me.' For God cannot be tempted by evil, nor does he tempt anyone; but each one is tempted when, *by his own evil desire*, he is dragged away and enticed. Then, after desire has conceived, it gives birth to sin; and sin, when it is full-grown, gives birth to death" (James 1:13–15, italics added).

Sin masters us in a four-step process: (1) we are beset by our own evil desires; (2) we are enticed by the world system; (3) the sin is acted out; (4) death sets in. In Shakespeare's *Julius Caesar*, Cassius says to Brutus, "The fault, dear Brutus, is not in our stars, but in ourselves, that we are underlings." For us, the problem of sin is not in our environment, but in ourselves. The integrity to understand and accept this reality personally is a major step to becoming a conqueror instead of a casualty.

CHOICES IN THE CONFLICT

A friend of mine once said, "Life is not made by the dreams we dream but by the choices we make." How true. Choices are the ingredients of triumph or failure.

When I was a pastor I received a note on my desk detailing the shocking story of a young man named Tom. He had been shot eight times as he sat on his motorcycle in front of a store in the Detroit area. The story went on to say that Tom was a member of the neo-Nazi motorcycle gang, "The Fourth Reich." What I read next was the sobering statement that his parents, now deceased, had been committed Christians and active members of our church. Tom had gone to our Sunday school, was saved and baptized in our fel-

lowship, and was active in the youth group. He had been removed
from our rolls fifteen years previously.

I leaned back in my chair and wondered how this could be.
Choices. That was the answer. Initially, it was not Tom's choice to
become a member of a violent gang. It would have been the furthest
thing from his mind when he was in our fellowship. Rather, it must
have been a series of small choices to rebel, to say no to God and
yes to his flesh and the system. Tom's choices veered him from the
path of righteousness and safety into the death of sin. Satan does
not captivate us. He simply capitalizes on our choices.

Sin awaits behind any number of choices we make: to lie to
gain personal advantage, to look a second and third time until we
plan that coveted affair, to carry out that dishonest business deal, to
refuse to forgive, to cheat on that test, to feed on pornography, to
escape through drugs, to ignore one's family, to put the priority of
Christ somewhere down the list—choices that seem so right and
feel so plausible. At the time, we may deem such choices as "necessary," yet they quickly usher us into the hands of the adversary and
the debilitating consequence of sin.

The conflict begins within, in response to the world without.
If we don't remain alert that the conflict is taking place, we can be
conquered through bad choices—sometimes without as much as a
whimper. Sadly, those who are conquered must live with the consequences.

CONSEQUENCES IN THE CONFLICT

"If you can get away with it, do it!"
"Everyone else is doing it!"
"Go ahead, God will still love you."
"Your parents won't punish you."
"God will forgive you."

These are our ways of suggesting that we can sin without consequence. While we cling to the promise of God's forgiveness
expressed in 1 John 1:9, we should also be aware of the warning,
"Do not be deceived: God cannot be mocked. A man reaps what he
sows. The one who sows to please his sinful nature, from that nature
will reap destruction; the one who sows to please the Spirit, from

the Spirit will reap eternal life" (Galatians 6:7–8).

Triumph in the kingdom conflict demands a clear understanding of consequence. God told Adam and Eve, and James concurs, that sin leads to death (Genesis 2:17; Romans 6:23; James 1:15). When Adam and Eve sinned, they immediately experienced death in several dimensions. Let's take a look at the consequences of their sin.

Death of Self-Esteem (Genesis 3:7)

Their perception of themselves totally changed. What once had been wonderful became a source of shame. They perceived their nakedness as negative; they were embarrassed and uncomfortable. Sin haunts us on the inside. We wonder, *What am I becoming? I never thought I would be this kind of person. If anyone knew this, they would reject me.* Sin destroys positive perceptions of who we are and what we are becoming.

Death of Integrity (Genesis 3:7)

Instead of dealing with their sin problem, Adam and Eve sought to cover it up. Fig leaves were their way of hiding their true condition and making themselves feel better. They no longer wanted to see themselves as they really were. We cleverly adorn ourselves with the fig leaves of excuses, rationalization, shifting of blame, comparing ourselves with those we feel are worse, procrastinating godliness, denying the reality of sin or the importance of God. These are the fig leaves of our "I'm OK, you're OK" covered-up society. Refusing to admit and deal with our true condition is a lack of reality, a loss of integrity. These fig leaves of sin are Satan's Band-Aids™ for the cancer of our true condition.

Death of Fellowship with God (Genesis 3:8)

When God appeared as usual, Adam and Eve withdrew from His presence! Instead of coming to Him in repentance, they hid from Him in shame. Sin keeps us from prayer, study of Scripture, and the fellowship of believers. It isolates us from our most important resources. In a Bible given to their son, parents wrote, "This book will keep you from sin, or sin will keep you from this book." How true.

Death of Personal Responsibility (Genesis 3:11–12)

God asked Adam if he had sinned; he replied that it was the woman's fault. Eve followed suit. How hard it is to admit we are wrong. Yet if we refuse to accept responsibility, we will sin and sin again. When we convince ourselves that it really isn't our fault, then the frequency of the offenses doesn't matter.

Sin results in spiritual and physical death. Broken relationships, emotional scars, lifelong memories, lost potential, habits that seem impossible to break, even suicide—all this and more are the consequences when we choose to sin.

But won't God forgive me? Absolutely. God is gracious, merciful, and forgiving. Forgiveness, however, doesn't necessarily erase consequences of sins already committed. Let's say that one Friday night after a hard week in the office I choose to stop at the local watering hole to drown my sorrows. After a couple of hours, I am stone drunk. I get into the car, weave toward home, hit the accelerator instead of the brake, and plow into a tree. My car is totaled and I land in the hospital where the doctors must amputate my leg. The next morning a friend visits me in the hospital and confronts me with my sin. I am broken! I beg God for forgiveness and He totally forgives me.

When dismissed from the hospital, I go to all the people I have offended: the bartender I insulted, the owner of the tree whose yard I landed in, and my friends and family members whom I have embarrassed with my actions. I beg their forgiveness and they too forgive me. I am fully forgiven, both by God and every person involved in my prior sin. But my leg will not grow back. Sin—even forgiven sin—has consequences, and I will live with the reminder of my sin throughout my life. Though God can even be glorified through the consequence, it remains with me as a lifelong limitation.

The kingdom conflict is real. It is fierce and the stakes are high. At stake are major issues like God's glory, our happiness, peace of mind, clear consciences, potential, the strength of the next generation, and the testimony of Christ in a dark and crooked world.

God's Word calls us to triumph. Peter warns us, "Be self-controlled and alert. Your enemy the devil prowls around like a roaring lion looking for someone to devour" (1 Peter 5:8). And Paul tells us in Ephesians 6:10–13 that the kingdom conflict is one of supernatural proportions:

> Finally, be strong in the Lord and in his mighty power. Put on the full armor of God so that you can take your stand against the devil's schemes. For our struggle is not against flesh and blood, but against the rulers, against the authorities, against the powers of this dark world and against the spiritual forces of evil in the heavenly realms. Therefore put on the full armor of God, so that when the day of evil comes, you may be able to stand your ground, and after you have done everything, to stand.

Though the conflict is supernatural in scope, God assures us of the potential for victory when He promises, "You, dear children, are from God and have overcome them, because the one who is in you is greater than the one who is in the world" (1 John 4:4).

How then can we actualize victory in this supernatural struggle? How can we become conquerors, not casualties? The first piece of spiritual armor is truth (Ephesians 6:14). Now that we have studied the truth about ourselves we must come to see the truth about the conflict from God's point of view. It is imperative that we permit His Word to unmask the adversary and expose the tragedy of his world system. Paul said, "If you forgive anyone, I also forgive him. And what I have forgiven . . . I have forgiven in the sight of Christ for your sake, *in order that Satan might not outwit us.* For we are not unaware of his schemes" (2 Corinthians 2:10–11, italics added). Paul's triumph over bitterness was rooted in an awareness of Satan's schemes. Therefore, Satan was not able to "outwit" him.

Coming to grips with Satan's strategy and the supernatural scope of the conflict is where we must begin. The Spirit will be our teacher, and Genesis will be our laboratory.

Questions for Your Personal Conflict

1. If you agree that no one is exempt from the powerful effect of sin, what specific actions do you take to minimize its influence on you?

2. During the past week, what excuses have you heard to explain or defend an offense against you? How did you respond to each excuse? How do you think God feels when we attempt to make excuses for sin rather than simply confessing and seeking forgiveness?

3. Can you think of any current situations in your life where you need to take the blame for something that has gone wrong? Are there situations where you need to take more responsibility? Do you need to ask someone's forgiveness for something you have done?

4. Read Ephesians 6:10–18, which describes the armor of God. Which of the pieces of armor would you say is weakest (or absent) in your life right now? Which would you say is your strongest characteristic?

5. What is one thing you are willing to do each day this week to minimize any potential alienation from God and get closer to Him?

2

KNOW YOUR ENEMY
The Battle Against Spiritual Blindness

When President Clinton decided to send U.S. troops into Bosnia, the biggest fear was not that they would be outnumbered or overpowered. The soldiers were well-trained and ready for battle. But the major concern of the U.S. military was the number of land mines they knew were hidden in the area. No matter how skilled a soldier might be, one careless step could be his last.

The first thing you ought to know about the kingdom conflict is that it isn't going to be a fair fight. On a level playing field with all the participants out in the open, it is clear that God and His followers will defeat those who oppose Him. From the first prophecy in Genesis 3:15 to the account of the final battle recorded in Revelation, the outcome of the kingdom conflict is a foregone conclusion. Those who put their trust in God will be victorious. Those who side with Satan will face defeat and judgment.

So the devil resorts to tactics that give him every possible edge. He uses deceit and lies, ambush and guerrilla warfare. No matter how prepared we are for battle, we must always be on our guard for covert agents and hidden dangers. His temptations are like land mines that threaten to go off at any time. We must always be prepared. Satan is a master at spiritual ambush who is able to defeat the unsuspecting and unprepared. Christians often are dreadfully naive.

If we are to emerge triumphant from the conflict, we must

peer through the smoke screen of this world system and see our adversary clearly. This is a challenging task because the battle to which we are called is beyond us; it is supernatural in scope. Paul describes the basis of Satan's system: "Our struggle is not against flesh and blood, but against the rulers, against the authorities, against the powers of this dark world and against the spiritual forces of evil in the heavenly realms" (Ephesians 6:12).

SEEING CLEARLY

A closer look at this verse and surrounding ones shows the triple threat of Satan's warfare: (1) crafty deceit; (2) supernatural power; and (3) personal injury.

Paul challenges us to use the whole armor of God in order to stand against the schemes of the devil (Ephesians 6:11). The word *schemes* means plans that are designed to deceive. This network of sin, the cosmos, is built on underhanded schemes that snare unsuspecting victims through *crafty* deceit.

My family heritage is rooted in a little town in Michigan which is known as the "magic capital of the world." Each summer an international convention of magicians is held in the village. We would vacation there, and, as a boy, I recall watching magicians do their tricks in the streets. I would stand in amazement! The performances looked so good, so awesome, so wonderful—until I learned to watch the magicians' hands and sleeves and notice what was going on behind their backs.

Satan's system is similar to a magic act. It is built on deceit and subtle seduction. It is more illusion than fact. As the King James Version translates Ephesians 6:11, it is a system full of the "wiles of the devil."

When it comes to sin, what you see is *not* what you get! When I fish, I always use bait to disguise the hook. So it is with Satan's system. He deceives us with the cultic sleight of hand that mixes truth with error.

My dad used to take our family to the circus. I was always intrigued by the sideshows. Great canvas posters promoted the thrill of seeing the bearded lady and the man with three arms. Yet my intense desire to pay the two-bit price and enjoy the experience was always squelched by my dad's assurance, "It is a waste of money." I grew up with one goal in mind—to see a circus sideshow. In time I had my chance, and how disappointing it was! Only too late did I realize Dad had been right and I had wasted my money. The posters *had* been far more alluring than the reality. Sin is like that, only it wastes lives, homes, potential, and peace.

Somehow we see more clearly *after* the sin is committed than before. While we're being tempted, sin seems enticing and worth any cost. Yet if we first put on the safety glasses of God's Word, we can see that temptation is actually crafty deceit. Scripture helps protect us against Satan, who seeks to take advantage of us.

Satan deceives us with the illusion that sin brings no consequences, that sin is fun for more than a season, that we can play with its fire and not get burned, and that it is just what we need and deserve.

A wise friend once advised me, "Never look at the temptation. Always look beyond it and see the tempter!" Looking at only the temptation is usually pleasing and alluring, but frequently ensures failure. We get a much clearer perspective by looking *beyond* the temptation itself to see the reality of the destructive consequences.

As Paul continues in Ephesians 6, he shows us that Satan's system is also one of *supernatural proportions*. We are up against a well-organized spiritual Mafia whose strength is beyond us. Ephesians 6:12 exposes a great chain of command with levels of demonic authority. It sobers me, almost frightens me, to realize that this well-organized system, supernatural in its power, is marshaled against my life. Is it any wonder that Paul predicates this exposé with a reminder to "be strong in the Lord and in his mighty power" (v. 10)? Satan's invisible, supernatural, extraterrestrial force is no fantasy. God says it's a reality. You and I are prone to its pressure. We live in the midst of it (John 17:14–18).

Current movies and television programming provide no shortage of demonic, supernatural themes. When we "entertain" ourselves with this devastating reality, we play a dangerous game. It desensitizes us to the reality of the danger.

Our struggle is beyond "flesh and blood." When your spouse puts you into a situation where you are tempted to become resentful, it is important to remember that your mate is not the ultimate issue. At issue is the supernatural power of darkness at work against your life. Your struggle is not really with your partner, but with the forces of sin that seek to devour you. Temptations that allure us are not the issue; they are merely the front, the bait, for extraterrestrial forces marshaled against our lives.

Paul's third exposure of Satan's system is that sin is like fiery darts that are hurled at us (Ephesians 6:16). The truth here is that *sin injures and defiles us.* Fiery darts have the potential of double damage. First is the pain caused by the puncture of the dart itself. But then the fire spreads damage to a much greater area. One person's failure often victimizes many others around him.

The ripples of sin are ugly and devastating. How clearly David saw and felt the injury after his sin with Bathsheba. He wrote:

> O Lord, do not rebuke me in your anger or discipline me in your wrath. For your arrows have pierced me, and your hand has come down upon me. Because of your wrath there is no health in my body; my bones have no soundness because of my sin. My guilt has overwhelmed me like a burden too heavy to bear. My wounds fester and are loathsome because of my sinful folly. I am bowed down and brought very low; all day long I go about mourning. My back is filled with searing pain; there is no health in my body. I am feeble and utterly crushed; I groan in anguish of heart. All my longings lie open before you, O Lord; my sighing is not hidden from you. My heart pounds, my strength fails me; even the light has gone from my eyes. My friends and companions avoid me because of my wounds; my neighbors stay far away. Those who seek my life set their traps, those who would harm me talk of my ruin; all day long they plot deception. (Psalm 38:1–12)

SEEING SATAN'S OBJECTIVE

Some people envision the kingdom conflict as a battle between two forces who love and desire us, each seeking our loyalty. Such people flatter themselves. Don't be fooled by this misperception. Satan doesn't desire your friendship, nor does he value you as a person. He is out for your ultimate demise. He simply wishes to use you to get to God.

Job is the classic example that reveals Satan's true objective. Satan approached God and accused Job of being righteous only because God had been good to him. Satan predicted that if God withheld His blessings, Job would "curse you to your face" (Job 1:9–11). In essence, Satan was slandering God's character in front of all the heavenly host. He was saying that God was not worthy of a man's allegiance in and of Himself; God had to "buy" man's love by blessing him.

To prove that people could faithfully worship Him regardless of their circumstances, God permitted Satan to take away all of Job's blessings. Family, health, wealth, friends, and happiness were stripped from him. Satan's goal was to diminish God's glory. He cared nothing for Job. In fact, he didn't mind wasting Job to accomplish his goal. Thankfully, Job was triumphant and demonstrated for all the universe that God was worthy of unconditional worship and allegiance. He glorified God.

Sin's ultimate objective is to destroy the glory and reputation of God! We were created in God's image (Genesis 1:26) for the purpose of reflecting His glory. Everything that God made was created to reflect what He is like, His glory. Yet all of creation has now been tarnished with the problem of sin (Romans 8:18–23).

Sin is Satan's graffiti on the wall of God's creation. Satan has taken God's perfect creation and filled it with greed, murder, selfishness, rape, disease, death, conflict, war, broken relationships, and lusts unchecked. Who gets blamed? God! How often we hear, "If God were good, why would all this be happening?" Satan has successfully injected misery into our experience to deface the image of God through us.

In junior high I sometimes found myself in the principal's office. He was a staunch Irish Catholic and I was the son of a Baptist minister. Of all his reproof, there was only one thing that always worked. If he really wanted to get through to me, all he had to say was, "Don't you know your behavior is a reflection on your parents?"

It is a sobering reality when I think that Satan attempts to make God look bad by affecting *my* behavior. It puts the cause into perspective and stimulates me to triumph, not so much for my own fulfillment, but for the reputation of God in and through my life! The world needs to see more clear reflections of God's glory. In fact, that is the reason He saved me. "Do you not know that your body is a temple of the Holy Spirit, who is in you, whom you have received from God? You are not your own; you were bought at a price. Therefore honor God with your body" (1 Corinthians 6:19–20).

SEEING GOD'S OBJECTIVE

Why would God create a mess like this in the first place? He didn't. He created a perfect environment and placed a perfect man and woman in it to bring glory to Him. Yet basic to this process was giving His creations the freedom of choice. God is not evil because He created choice. Choice was necessary in order for genuine worship and love to abound.

The choice to worship and submit to God revolved around a single command: "You are free to eat from any tree in the garden; but you must not eat from the tree of the knowledge of good and evil, for when you eat of it you will surely die" (Genesis 2:16–17). Obeying this command was Adam and Eve's opportunity to demonstrate their love for God, to freely choose to worship God and glorify His worthiness to be their Lord. Had they been created without choice, they would be little more than robots. God's worthiness to be worshiped would not be served, because forced fellowship proves nothing.

God's objective for our experience is shown in Genesis 1:26–30:

> Then God said, "Let us make man in our image, in our likeness, and let them rule over the fish of the sea and the birds of the air, over the livestock, over all the earth, and over all the creatures that move along the ground." So God created man in his own image, in the image of God he created him; male and female he created them. God blessed them and said to them, "Be fruitful and increase in number; fill the earth and subdue it. Rule over the fish of the sea and the birds of the air and over every living creature that moves on the ground." Then God said, "I give you every seed-bearing plant on the face of the whole earth and every tree that has fruit with seed in it. They will be yours for food. And to all the beasts of the earth and all the birds of the air and all the creatures that move on the ground—everything that has the breath of life in it—I give every green plant for food."

In this passage, the order for joy and fulfillment is established. It begins with God being Lord over man, the image-bearer, and man serving God by being lord over creation.

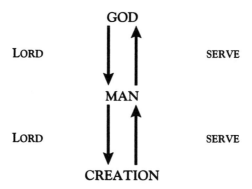

Serving God and controlling creation is the God-designed "fulfillment factor" for living. It means that God unconditionally manages my life. Being committed to Him as the only Lord of my life, I never permit my environment to control me; I experience lordship over it. I never yield my life to anything in this world but, rather, subdue the world around me and use it to glorify my God. It is the privilege and responsibility of taking dominion over God's creation.

In this pattern I refuse to become a servant to a bank account, a car, a body, a house, a job, or anything else in my environment. Jehovah is my Lord. He manages my life. I manage my environment to His glory. For Adam and Eve, the tree in the midst of their environment (2:17) was the opportunity to demonstrate their commitment to this fulfillment factor.

This divine order reflects God's perfect plan for us and the universe. This order not only glorifies God, but also gives man dignity and clear fellowship with his Creator. It establishes man as the highest entity of God's creation, the governor of the created order. It guarantees that the material world will be subject to the higher world of spiritual realities and that the material world will mirror the glory of God.

So what happened? How did man wander from the joy of this fulfillment factor?

SEEING THE FALL

Tragically, God's divine plan, the fulfillment factor, was invaded by Satan and has been entirely reordered. We have said that Satan uses "crafty deceit." Genesis 3:1 confirms that "the serpent was more crafty than any of the wild animals the Lord God had made." Satan, in the form of the serpent, approached Eve in her perfect environment of Eden and appealed to her freedom of choice—the freedom that God had given her. It wasn't long before she succumbed to his temptation.

> When the woman saw that the fruit of the tree was good for food and pleasing to the eye, and also desirable for gaining wisdom, she took some and ate it. She also gave some to her husband, who was with her, and he ate it. Then the eyes of both of them were opened, and they realized they were naked; so they sewed fig leaves together and made coverings for themselves. (Genesis 3:6–7)

Satan has turned the tables. He has used the tree and its fruit (creation) to subdue and capture the governors of the world. Man is now serving Satan by serving creation. God's place is completely gone. Creation controls man.

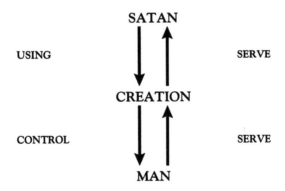

That, literally, was the night the lights went out in Eden. Satan, by capturing the governors of this world, established himself as the prince of this world, the god of this world, the prince of the power of the air (John 12:31; 2 Corinthians 4:4; Ephesians 2:2). Sin entered the scene and defiled Adam, Eve, and all of creation, the very instrument of God's glory (Romans 8:20–22). These reordered relationships continue today as the basic flow of Satan's world system.

Satan *uses* creation (the tree) to entice man into his control. Man submits to the alluring creation and in so doing serves Satan. God is expelled from experience.

This new "fallen factor" permeates everything godless man does. Tragically, it is even reflected in the behavior of some believers. Creation, in the form of silver, gold, cars, houses, bodies, vacation spots, and every material portion of the universe, lures us to live for *it* and to sacrifice values of godliness to satisfy our unchecked desires. This fallen factor places the material over the spiritual. It degrades us, and it brings death and Satan's defilement to our environment and experience.

This pattern is seen in the husband and father who neglects his family for the accumulation of material (created) things, the wife who destroys her relationship to her home and her Lord by having an affair, or the student who willingly sacrifices spiritual potential by choosing to prepare only for those occupations that make him rich rather than considering what God would have him do. The fallen factor exerts its influence on those who can no longer give their resources to God's work because they have spent their discretionary income to drive better cars and live in better places. Satan still uses creation to lure us to serve him. In so doing we deny God and His glory through us.

SEEING THE STRATEGY: ALIENATION

How was Satan able to so completely overthrow the fulfillment factor, the plan and program of God? He used one of the most powerful strategies in his arsenal—the process of alienation.

Genesis 3 records a step-by-step process that alienated Eve both mentally and emotionally from God. She began in a perfect environment where she, Adam, God, and creation lived in unhindered joy and fellowship—an environment where man had dignity and the spiritual world flooded the material world with God's glory. There was only one point of vulnerability; God had given man and woman the freedom of choice! Satan's task was to somehow condition Eve to choose to serve him and rebel against God. He had to diminish her love, respect, and ultimately her allegiance to Jehovah.

Think Wrongly About God and His Word

The first step of alienation began with Satan influencing Eve to think wrongly about God and His Word. Satan said to her, "Did God really say, 'You must not eat from any tree in the garden'?" (Genesis 3:1). This misleading question caused her to perceive God as being restrictive and stingy. What God had actually said was, "You must not eat from the tree of the knowledge of good and evil, for when you eat of it you will surely die" (2:17). She could eat from *all* the trees but one. How generous! Satan fed misinformation about God and His Word to lead Eve to believe that God was less than good, and that He gave her commands to restrict her freedom. She began to feel alienated from this God who suddenly seemed rather narrow and confining. Her love for Him was diminished.

Deny the Consequences of Disobedience

The second stage of alienation is to deny the consequences of disobedience. In the process of answering Satan, Eve stated that if she ate the fruit she would die. Sin and disobedience would separate her from God, the life source. Satan immediately countered with his second lie. He said, "You will not surely die" (3:4). If there is no consequence to sin, then why not enjoy it?

Deny That God Cares for His People

Underlying the denial of consequence is the third stage of alienation, which in essence is to deny that God really cares for His people. Satan explained to Eve, "God knows that when you eat of it your eyes will be opened, and you will be like God, knowing good and evil" (3:5). Satan's lies are accusatory: that God cares only for Himself . . . that His commands keep us from enjoying the fullness of life and from becoming like Him . . . that He really doesn't care for us . . . that He uses His commands to restrict our pleasure and manipulate us into obedience by intimidating us with empty threats.

Once Eve began to believe these false accusations of Satan, the wedge of alienation was driven into what before had been a relationship of joy and fulfillment. Her love and respect for God were now diminished. Her allegiance was up for grabs.

Satan still uses the same modus operandi. He tells us these same lies to separate our hearts from God. He gets us to see God as a capricious old Man in the sky who is like a pair of celestial hand-cuffs. God's Word is perceived as a heavenly straitjacket, old-fashioned to say the least. Satan consistently denies consequence. He capitalizes on crisis to seduce us into thinking that God doesn't care. If God cared, why did He create me this way? Why did my parents divorce? Why am I still single?

Once Eve was alienated from God and His truth, she saw the tree in a new light (3:6). It now appealed to her as good—good for food, good as an object of beauty, and good for her future. It appeared to be her ticket to wisdom.

Satan ultimately seeks to use what God says is evil and make it seem good. When alienated from God, we fail to see clearly. We become dreadfully vulnerable to Satan's ambush. Captured. Prisoners of a supernatural warfare.

Questions for Your Personal Conflict

1. If Satan wanted to hook you into committing a sin, what "bait" would be most effective to get your attention?

2. Try to recall the last time you became involved in a sin because you weren't prepared. How can you avoid being "ambushed" in a similar way in the future?

3. Recall the last three fights or arguments you had. In each case, can you determine a deeper problem beneath the stated issues?

4. Read Job 1–2 and 42. If you had been in Job's place, do you think you would have withstood his entire period of testing? If not, at what point do you think you would have cracked? What did Job learn from the experience? What can we learn from it?

5. What are some specific actions you can take this week to replace your natural "fallen factor" with the "fulfillment factor" that only God can provide?

3

WE THREE KINGDOMS
Choosing Wisely for Whom You Will Fight

Do you ever take a good look at people coming into an office on Monday morning? The cups of espresso picked up on the way are long gone, so they stumble to the coffee machine and return to their desks clutching their fresh caffeine, staring blankly into space with a look of torment etched on their faces. No one dares to even pose the question: "Are you happy to be here this morning?"

Since getting to work after a delightful weekend is so much trouble, why do they go to all that effort? Why do they torture themselves? They'll tell you they do it for Friday—payday. They go through the suffering and hard work each day in the perspective of the ultimate outcome. All the misery of Monday mornings somehow seems worthwhile as we look back on Fridays.

In the workplace we see the value of being "bigger-picture" people. We need to learn to do the same as we consider the kingdom conflict. If I perceive that the struggle with sin is simply a matter between myself and the devil, my outlook is both limited and dangerous.

There is a bigger picture that consists of a supernatural struggle. The kingdom conflict is being waged this moment on our planet. Earth is the theater of war and our minds and our hearts are the battlefields. To better understand this struggle, we need to consider three kingdoms: (1) the kingdom of Satan; (2) the kingdom of Christ; and (3) the theocratic kingdom.

THE KINGDOM OF SATAN

Satan established his kingdom when he introduced the "fallen factor" by seducing Adam and Eve into choosing to serve him instead of God (Genesis 3). Mankind's choice to follow Satan rather than God introduced sin and its devastation into the human form, creation, and the universe (Romans 8). Satan knew that if he captured man, he would have control over the governors of creation and could set himself up as the god of this world (2 Corinthians 4:4). Since mankind and creation were the glory of God, the introduction of sin and the satanic forces into creation would deface His glory and give Satan a continuing base of operation against Him. At this point, our planet, Earth, became the domain of Satan and the focal point of this conflict.

Earth is identified as the domain of Satan throughout Scripture (Job 1:7; Matthew 4:8–9; John 16:11; 2 Corinthians 4:4; Ephesians 2:2). The earth is governed by a system of sin and godlessness. Importantly, you and I are targeted to become captives of this sinful system (Ephesians 6:10–18; 1 Peter 5:8).

What will God do now? His creation has been victimized by the rebel angelic host, and His glory is at stake in the universe. He could annihilate everything, but that would do nothing to enhance the glory of His love and grace. How then can He restore His glory to creation? How can man again find dignity and worth? How can God best express His grace, mercy, forgiveness, righteousness, holiness, and justice?

THE KINGDOM OF CHRIST

God's strategy was to reveal His glory in a fallen universe through redemption . . . rescue . . . a master plan to free the hostages of sin to once again fellowship with Him and reflect His glory! He would accomplish this by establishing a kingdom that would ultimately defeat the kingdom of Satan. The Bible calls it the kingdom of Christ.

This kingdom would be established around a Man who would live a perfect life within the sinful system of Satan to demonstrate that holiness can prevail (Hebrews 4:15). This Man would die for the sins of all so that God's justice could be served (Romans 5:1). He would offer restoration with God through His sacrificial death so that both love and grace might be magnified (John 3:16; Ephesians 1:6). Through resurrection He would conquer death, the ultimate stroke of sin, which would affirm and reveal the victorious power of God (1 Corinthians 15:51–57; Philippians 3:10). This King would then sit in judgment on both the corrupted system of Satan and Satan himself, finally banishing Satan eternally from the universe to reveal God's righteousness (Revelation 20). Ultimately, this King would destroy the sin-tainted universe and create a new heaven and a new earth that would forever be populated by those who are locked into eternal righteousness, unable now to sin because they have chosen redemption (Revelation 21).

This plan brings ultimate glory to God. It also offers to mankind, whom He loves, the opportunity to once again, now and forever, enjoy the intended pleasures of Eden. The fallen factor is replaced by God's originally intended fulfillment factor.

What Man would qualify to so glorify God and guarantee the rescue of mankind from the destructive bondage of sin? None of us could possibly be counted on. God, in the ultimate demonstration of His love, came Himself in the form of a Man to accomplish the task. His name was Jesus, literally *Savior*. Consequently, it is His kingdom that will ultimately prevail (Philippians 2:9–11; 1 Corinthians 15:20–27). The purpose of the kingdom of Christ is to defeat the kingdom of Satan and to present to the Father the finished victory. This victory has been assured through the Resurrection and now awaits consummation based on God's timetable (1 Corinthians 15:55–57; 1 John 4:4).

This kingdom of Christ's is more than a matter of theology. For believers, it is an intricate and profound reality of our experience. "For he has rescued us from the dominion of darkness and brought us into the kingdom of the Son he loves" (Colossians 1:13). We are kingdom people . . . soldiers in Christ's army (2 Timothy 2:3). Though we continue to dwell in Satan's domain (John 17:14–15), we are uniquely different (2 Corinthians 5:17), reflecting the glory of God in the face of Satan's system (1 Corinthians 6:19–20; 2 Corinthians 3:18). That is why Satan so tenaciously seeks to devour us.

Christians are walking, talking testimonies to the victorious kingdom of Christ (2 Corinthians 3:2–3; 5:20). We represent Satan's defeat and his subservience to Christ the King. That's exactly why Christ prayed that we should remain *in* the world but not *of* the world, set apart by the truth lived through us. As kingdom people we are used by Christ to bring others into His kingdom, thus glorifying God (John 17:14–21).

The kingdom of Christ, to which we pledge allegiance, has a history battered by the all-out hostility of the forces of hell. Satan hates the kingdom of Christ. It represents his final and permanent demise.

The announcement that Christ's kingdom would enter the domain of Satan to fulfill its rescue operation is found as early as Genesis 3:15. In judging Satan, God says, "I will put enmity between you and the woman, and between your offspring and hers; he will crush your head, and you will strike his heel." Though Satan will strike a near-fatal blow (the Crucifixion) to the seed of woman, that seed (Jesus Christ) will deliver a fatal blow to Satan and his domain.

Genesis 3:15 is Christ's kingdom in germinal form. It is a call to arms. This is the first announcement of the Messiah, and Satan hears every word. The battle lines are drawn. As far as Satan is concerned, any righteous seed of woman may very well be the promised victor. Satan will do everything in his power to prevent this prophecy from coming true. It now becomes Satan's goal to annihilate the Messiah seed.

The Messiah seed is traced through the Old Testament from Adam to Noah to Abraham to Israel (Jacob) to David and ultimately, as the prophets prophesied, to Christ. The Old Testament is a history of Satan's continual attacks on the Messiah seed, his attempt to prevent the coming kingdom of Christ. The New Testament describes the triumph of the Messiah on earth through the church.

In the Old Testament, it was Satan's purpose to deny victory to the kingdom of Christ by thwarting its arrival. And in the New Testament, after the Messiah finally arrived, the Cross became

Satan's ultimate stroke. That was his best hour. He had finally snuffed out the promise and defeated the One sent to defeat him. All of hell rejoiced . . . for three days. Then the glory of God's ultimate and omnipotent power was displayed for us to see as Christ rose again, defeating Satan permanently (John 16:11; 1 Corinthians 15:20–28).

While it was the responsibility of the Old Testament saints to preserve the Messiah seed, it is now our privilege to promote the victorious Messiah message. Since Satan was unsuccessful in preventing the establishment of the kingdom of Christ, his revised strategy is to use his power to diminish the message and deface the Messiah's glory through us.

Satan is like a rowdy kid who has been wrestled to the ground and is being held there by another boy who has beaten him. Full of hatred and anger, the boy on his back spits in the face of his victorious foe. He's down, but not out. It is Satan's delight to spit in God's face by conquering us as God's people and destroying the glory of the Messiah message by leading us into sin.

I recall watching a chicken being butchered in a barnyard. As you may know, once its head is cut off there is no hope, yet it runs around the barnyard, headless, in a flurry of feathers, blood, and dust. Then, just as quickly, it falls over dead. Likewise, Satan has already been defeated. But until his sentencing is actualized (Revelation 20:10), he seeks to brutalize God's glory in a hellish flurry of activity in the barnyard of the world. Since we live in the world for the glory of God, the conflict is waged in the territory of our hearts, minds, bodies, and relationships.

THE THEOCRATIC KINGDOM

Were it not for the third kingdom in this conflict, we might very well be concerned that somehow Satan's domain could ultimately conquer us. Take heart. Overseeing this struggle is what theologians often term the theocratic kingdom. A *theocracy* is a government led by immediate divine guidance. God's sovereign rule guarantees that in the end His plan and purpose will be triumphant.

Here are just a few references to the certainty of God's theocratic kingdom:

- "Lift up your heads, O you gates; be lifted up, you ancient doors, that the King of glory may come in. Who is this King of glory? The Lord strong and mighty, the Lord mighty in battle. . . . Who is he, this King of glory? The Lord Almighty —he is the King of glory" (Psalm 24:7–8, 10).
- "For God is the King of all the earth; sing to him a psalm of praise" (Psalm 47:7).
- "The Lord has established his throne in heaven, and his kingdom rules over all" (Psalm 103:19).
- "The king's heart is in the hand of the Lord; he directs it like a watercourse wherever he pleases" (Proverbs 21:1).

The theocratic kingdom is also referred to in Psalms 10:16; 29:10; and 95:3; Daniel 4:34–35; 1 Timothy 1:17; and 1 Corinthians 15:24–28.

In our lives we will certainly face momentary despair. As we shall see, throughout Scripture it often seems that Satan's kingdom has prevailed. In every instance, however, God theocratically intervenes and ultimately demonstrates the surety of His plan.

The introduction of the theocratic kingdom comes as early as the third chapter of Genesis. Satan has just established his domain, and God's rule has been banished from the face of the earth. Man, now a sinner, has no desire to fellowship with or please God. Yet as soon as these tragic events take place, God theocratically intervenes to reorder creation and to pronounce His redemptive plan through the kingdom of Christ. Note the pattern of God's theocratic intervention.

Confrontation (Genesis 3:8–14)

God confronts Eve, Adam, and Satan with their rebellion against Him. As sinners, Adam and Eve hid from God. God, in the fullness of His grace and love, took the initiative and called them to come to Him—even while in their sinful condition. It is no different today when the voice of the Savior tugs at the heart of a sinner hidden in the bushes of his fallen condition, or of a believer whose willful sin has driven a wedge in the relationship between himself and God. God incessantly, penetratingly, lovingly calls us to Himself. It is His purposeful intervention.

Consequence (Genesis 3:14–19)

Sin *always* has consequence. Even forgiveness does not always erase the sting of sin's consequence. Now that sin has become a part of man's experience, everything must be rearranged. These judgments of Genesis 3:14–19 are the consequence of man's choice and are necessary to the new order of life in a world under the dominion of sin. God theocratically judges sin.

Promise (Genesis 3:15–20)

Adam believed God's promise that victory would come through the seed of the woman (v. 15), and he named his wife accordingly (v. 20). That act of faith in response to God's promise of the Messiah is the key to restoration. Throughout Scripture, actualized faith in God's promise of redemption is the basis for man's salvation (Ephesians 2:8–9). God intervenes to promise something better than Satan's domain offers.

Restoration (Genesis 3:21)

In restoring them to fellowship with Himself, God could not accept Adam and Eve's self-made covering for sin. The fig leaves were discarded. God shed the blood of an animal and clothed Adam and Eve with the animal's skin. It is God and God alone who can cover and cancel the shame of our sins (Titus 3:5). This act of love by God symbolized forgiveness and restoration for Adam and Eve. It may also have been the institution of sacrifices for sin through the blood of animals.

Safety (Genesis 3:22–24)

God, in His theocratic intervention, frequently and mercifully imposes parameters so that we don't make matters worse for ourselves. In this case, God protected Adam and Eve from eating of the tree of life and living forever in sin. It at first seems cruel to expel them from the garden and post cherubs brandishing flaming swords to prevent them from reentering. But if Adam and Eve had eaten from the tree of life, they would have been eternally locked into their sin-hindered condition. God had a better plan—ultimate redemption through the kingdom of Christ. Adam would someday be without sin, totally released from its influence and able to enjoy righteousness. The guarded garden was an act of God's mercy to keep Adam and Eve safe from themselves.

By the end of Genesis 3, God had theocratically begun to repair His fallen world and to guarantee ultimate victory. God cared enough to sovereignly intrude into the mess His people had made in order to rescue His hopeless creatures and reestablish His glory. It is the theocratic kingdom's first thrust into the conflict. Satan had won the battle; God would win the war.

The ultimate, assured theocratic victory of our Almighty God stands as the final recourse for our confidence, courage, and comfort. We are surely on the victorious side. With this perspective, willful sin in the believer's life becomes absurd.

The ancient Chinese used to have an interesting way to stage their dramas. Their theaters were built so that the audience could see two levels. Actors on the first level would portray the ongoing scheme of the play, while on the second level the conclusion to the drama was portrayed. When the hero on the first level was about to give up to the villain in hopeless despair, the crowd would yell for him to persevere because they could see that in the end he would prevail.

So it is with us. God has revealed on the second level the reality of the ultimate triumph of His glory. The kingdom of Christ will prevail, guaranteed by the sovereign intervention of the theocratic kingdom. We should cheer each other on to persevere. We should encourage one another to actualize that victory as we live in Satan's domain. As we perform on the first-level stage of Satan's domain, our victory is already settled and sure. We can be triumphant for God's glory. We can walk with Him, act out His plot, and speak the lines He gives us. As we do, He will often theocratically, supernaturally intervene to accomplish His glory through us so that we might affirm, "Now to the King eternal, immortal, invisible, the only God, be honor and glory for ever and ever. Amen" (1 Timothy 1:17).

SATAN'S STRATEGY UNMASKED

Through the course of biblical history this kingdom conflict has revealed the strategies of Satan. Satan uses specific tactics, executed with great precision, to attack the kingdom of Christ. Too often his tactics are successful. As Paul said, we dare not be ignorant of Satan's devices lest he take advantage of us (2 Corinthians 2:11). Some people suggest that ignorance is bliss. In legal matters, ignorance of the law is no excuse. But when it comes to this great kingdom struggle in our soul, ignorance spells certain defeat.

The book of Genesis is especially graphic in exposing Satan's strategies and his attacks on the Messiah seed. Interestingly, Satan still attacks our lives using those very same tactics. Is his arsenal limited? No. It's simply that the same strategy works over and over again. As long as a football team's offensive strategy is scoring points against their opponents, they aren't likely to change it. It's up to the other team to take note and make the necessary changes on *defense*. Someone once said that it is a wise person who learns from others' mistakes. It is a victorious believer who learns the lessons of history and arms himself or herself accordingly.

In the chapters that follow, we will take a closer look at Satan's favorite strategies. Against Eve, he used lies about God to drive a wedge of alienation into her heart. Against Cain, he used the urge to live for oneself. Against the people of Noah's time, he used the seduction of outward beauty that led to intermarriage with the ungodly. Against the people after the flood at Babel, he used self-glory. Against Abraham, he used fear. Against Sarah, impatience. Against Esau, the urge for the instant gratification brought about by material goods. Satan still uses these same successful tactics to separate people from the truth and goodness of God.

All these strategies were directed at the Messiah seed, the kingdom of Christ, through God's chosen people. We should learn from the mistakes of these people, as well as from the victories of those who overcame Satan's strategies. Joseph, for example, stood tall for God and provided sharp contrast with others who were toppled by the onslaught of Satan's supernatural system—even while he was fraught with discouragement. We fortify ourselves by learning from the lives of such people.

Seeing our lives in the scope of the extraterrestrial, supernatural kingdom conflict motivates us to succeed on Christ's behalf for the cause of His kingdom. As we live out God's plan, we do so staring into the teeth of Satan's domain. Our confidence and courage are found in the reality of God's ultimate, sovereignly guaranteed, theocratically arranged victory.

Questions for Your Personal Conflict

1. Although Christians don't belong to the kingdom of Satan, what are some of the things we do that might be considered "fraternizing with the enemy"?

2. Think of a situation where you are responsible for a group of people (as their boss at work, a Scout leader or youth sponsor, etc.). What do you expect of those under your leadership? As one of the members of the kingdom of Christ, in what ways do you reflect the same qualities you expect of others?

3. The fact that God is a theocratic leader—acting as He sees fit—suggests that He will not always appear to be fair by your definition. How do you stand to benefit from being part of God's theocracy? What complaints, if any, might you have from time to time?

4. Read 1 Corinthians 10:12–13. As you find yourself engaged in the kingdom conflict, what are some things you need to keep in mind?

5. Can you think of a specific example how the kingdom conflict takes place in each of the following territories:
   - Your heart?
   - Your mind?
   - Your body?
   - Your relationships?

4

THE CONFLICT WITH SELF
The Battle Within

Our culture shamelessly flaunts the importance of "self." Since the 1960s we have been rearing and reaping what sociologists call the "ME" generation. Self-centeredness is nothing new; it just finally came out of the closet. Recent generations simply have had the integrity to admit that they want and are dedicated to get what's best for themselves.

When it comes to contract negotiating time in professional baseball, football, and basketball, it's hard to believe that these are supposedly *team* sports. "Star" individuals frequently make monetary demands that strain both the budget of the owners and the comprehension of those who read about it. Sometimes a player will make demands simply to become the highest paid person in his sport. If the team he is "loyal" to refuses to pay, he doesn't think twice about signing with another one that will. Then, on top of such incomprehensible salaries and additional millions in endorsement opportunities, some of the same people still refuse to sign autographs for young loyal fans without charging for it. They are out for what they can get while they can get it, and they don't mind who knows.

The same mentality permeates society at almost all levels. How often do you hear about an accident without some kind of lawsuit that follows immediately? Recently a woman sued a nine-year-old boy because he had hit a foul ball at a little league game which had struck her. The papers were served at his home, and he was quite shaken up about it.

Millions of unborn babies have been murdered basically because we don't want them. A national news magazine, in its story on abortion in America, concluded by stating that the two prevailing reasons for abortion were the health and/or the happiness of the mother.

I have spoken with numerous people in the process of leaving their spouses, simply because the allure of another love affair was strong. The consequences to others—the rejected husband or wife, kids, families involved, Christian testimony—just don't seem to matter. Neither do the potential consequences to the person involved, such as alienation from God, guilt, or regrets and insecurity that must be dealt with in the future. All that seems to matter to these people is the here-and-now opportunity to feed the hunger of self-centeredness.

The adults of today grew up with numerous themes appealing to self: "You owe it to yourself. . . . Do your own thing. . . . Look out for number one. . . . You only go round once, so go for the gusto. . . . Stand up for your rights. . . . You deserve a break today." With enough time and repetition, it all begins to sound logical and make sense. We believe we *do* deserve more than we're receiving. And like pro athletes, we start to make whatever demands we think we can get by with.

To the believer who seeks to triumph for God, it is essential to know that all of sin—all of our spiritual failure—begins with this thing called *self*. Doing what pleases *me*, at the expense of what pleases God, is the first step away from Him.

Immorality, idolatry, destructive talk, envy, anger, jealousy, hatred—they all find their source in the problem of self. The chubby little hand that quickly transfers a candy bar into his pocket at the store is responding to self-centeredness. So is the hand that fills out the form that shortchanges the IRS.

Lucifer said, "I will be like God!" (Isaiah 14:14). Eve saw that the fruit of the forbidden tree would be good for her. And in this chapter we will see that Cain wanted to worship his way. Self is the continuing thread as the story of Satan's kingdom unravels throughout the narrative of Genesis.

For Adam and Eve, life revolved around a promise that a Child would be born to defeat the sin-damaged system they had created for themselves (Genesis 3:15). For Satan, success would depend on making sure that promise never came true. Since Satan did not know who the Child would be, every righteous seed of woman was suspect, and as such, would be the focus of attack by the system of this world.

As we move into Genesis 4, we will see that Abel serves God, but Cain is dedicated to self. By the end of the chapter, Satan has used Cain's selfishness to extinguish the righteous seed. A secular, godless, violent civilization defaces the glory of God's creation (4:17–24). There is no one to fulfill the promise of the Messiah. The kingdom of Christ has no bloodline.

THE SELF-STYLED LIFESTYLE

Cain proves that the problem of self is as old as human history and is a major strategy used effectively by Satan. Cain's actions reveal the sad process of a self-styled lifestyle.

Cain's selfishness was first exposed through a religious encounter. Cain came to worship God, bringing the kind of sacrifice that he wanted to bring. God did not accept his sacrifice and gave Cain another opportunity to bring an acceptable offering. Whether it was a wrong kind of sacrifice, the wrong attitude in bringing the sacrifice, or both, the point is that Cain's worship was unacceptable to God (Genesis 4:3–7).

Cain didn't mind worshiping and serving God. He just wanted to do it *his* way. Self-styled religion was Satan's first attack on the kingdom of Christ. Most of us, like Cain, want to come to God on our own terms. Liberal theology seeks to make God comfortable and convenient. Cults seek to use worship to elevate human personalities. Many religions accumulate layers upon layers of tradition that satisfy the wants of their constituency. Most important, within biblically framed systems of worship, there are believers who pick and choose the elements of the creed that will benefit them while ignoring the more demanding requirements of true discipleship. Many believers really don't care much what the Bible says about their lifestyles—we are prone to stubbornly do what we want to do. In this light, we are not much different than Cain.

God is absolute. We must worship and serve Him on His terms (John 4:24). Any worship that is not in the scope of His requirements will be rejected, regardless of how sincere, well-meaning, or logical the ceremony might be.

Yet God is also gracious. When our worship becomes self-serving and off the true mark, He gives us the opportunity to repent and serve Him appropriately. God gave Cain a second chance (Genesis 4:7). Yet Cain refused to conform to God's plan. He stubbornly affirmed his selfish choice.

SELF: ITS OWN WORST ENEMY

Cain demonstrates the pattern of a self-styled lifestyle. Selfishness, though seemingly the way to fulfillment, leads to a whole system of despair that Satan uses to defeat the glory of God through us. Let's take a closer look at the flow of the self-styled lifestyle.

Self-Determination (Genesis 4:3)

Cain didn't mind looking religious. He just wanted to reserve the right to determine his religion and how he exercised it. The central issue of all of life is who will be boss. That issue often comes to rest at the crossroads where God and His will meet me and my life, dreams, and desires. Like Cain, I want to determine my own way of living. It's OK if God wants to come along, but in reality, "I will call the shots."

Stubbornness (Genesis 4:4–7)

So tenacious was Cain in his commitment to self that he refused God's offer of a second chance. He was not interested in changing. Once self has determined a course of life, it often becomes entrenched. I'm reminded of Jonah, who was willing to die rather than obey God (Jonah 1:12). Selfishness often matures into an unreasonable stubbornness that only compounds the ultimate misery.

Anger (Genesis 4:5–6)

The fallacy of selfishness is that we try to implement it in an environment full of other people and responsibilities. If we lived alone on an island and if there were no God, self-centeredness might be a workable option. However, selfishness always conflicts with the lives of others and our responsibilities toward God. When we act selfishly, reproof is imminent. The reproof may come in the form of a broken relationship or a verbal encounter with an authority figure or associate. For believers, it often comes from God and His Word.

So it was with Cain. God reproved Cain, and Cain didn't like it. People committed to self-fulfillment rarely appreciate it when their selfishness is pointed out and criticized. So like a stubborn child, Cain developed an angry spirit. It showed on his face (Genesis 4:5–6). His anger, though unjustified, became an all-consuming drive within him. Selfish people are angry people and are therefore prone to more serious problems, including bitterness, hatred, and the attendant destruction of self and others. When Jonah selfishly wanted Ninevah destroyed and didn't get his way, he became so angry that he threatened suicide (Jonah 4:1–3).

Vulnerability (Genesis 4:7)

People committed to self-fulfillment are most vulnerable to the problem of sin. God warned Cain that if he chose to maintain his commitment to self, sin would literally be like a beast crouching at the threshold of his life; he would spend his life struggling to conquer it. This warning was a clear statement from God that selfishness breeds sinfulness.

Hatred (Genesis 4:8)

Rather than being repentant, or even angry at himself for his failure to please God, Cain's anger was vented toward Abel. By refusing his second chance, Cain had *chosen* to be rejected, and Abel represented what was right: the dedication of self to God. Abel was accepted by God. Abel was a walking reminder to Cain of his self-centered disobedience! Cain hated Abel for no better reason than because Abel's goodness was a bad reflection on him.

Murder (Genesis 4:8)

Unable to tolerate this symbol of his sin, Cain killed Abel. This murder may be the first thing we think of when we recall the Cain and Abel story. Yet it becomes more significant when we see this vile action in the context of a process. When we don't deal with self-determination, it becomes anger. When we don't deal with anger, it grows into hatred. When we don't deal with hatred, it may even result in murder.

Jesus makes this same observation in His Sermon on the Mount (Matthew 5:21–26). The earlier we begin to deal with the problem, the easier it is to do something about it. Because Cain failed to do so, his commitment to self was used by Satan to extinguish the righteous seed of woman, therefore protecting Satan's grip on this world.

Loss of Integrity (Genesis 4:9)

Sin spreads quickly. One sin usually leads to many others, especially in cases where we try to cover up what we have done. After Cain had committed cold-blooded murder, what was a little lie to him? Lying is a way of life for those who are committed to self. Once self has acted out its sin, it needs a mechanism for protection and self-defense. Lying becomes that ally.

Judgment and Sorrow (Genesis 4:10–15)

Cain learned the hard way that sin will not go unpunished forever. Perhaps he thought no one would ever avenge the murder. Yet God went to Cain and judged him for his sin. In response, Cain collapsed in sorrow. The consequences of his selfishness suddenly seemed more than he could bear. He hadn't planned on having to account for his action. Selfishness inevitably leads to immense misery, for it alienates us from our major sources of joy and fulfillment—God and friends. It creates a crushing feeling of helplessness.

Fear (Genesis 4:14)

Immediately, Cain expressed fear that now he would be killed by someone else. Self-centeredness makes us suspicious and afraid. A businessperson who cheats his competitors has a great fear of being cheated, and he imposes that suspicion on his relationships.

A gossiper suspects that others gossip about him. An unfaithful marriage partner has a heightened suspicion about the marital loyalty of his mate. Fear and suspicion change the atmosphere of our relationships from openness and integrity to insecurity and doubt.

False Security (Genesis 4:16–24)

God told Cain to be a wanderer and a fugitive on the earth. Instead, Cain again asserted himself against God and established a city. By grouping people around him who were likewise dedicated to self (Genesis 3:23–24), Cain provided a false network of security. Though his culture was becoming technologically advanced, it was unashamedly evil. It was a city full of violence. Another man named Lamech boasted of two murders (4:23). Self-centered people tend to group together and encourage one another in their selfish ways.

STILL THE SAME

Cain's commitment to a self-styled lifestyle, though religious, led to God's reproof. Choosing to reject the reproof, Cain played into the scheme of Satan. The natural results of his selfishness eliminated the righteous seed (Abel) and established a sophisticated culture of self-centered sinners who were in the process of destroying one another.

Scientific gain, great cities, and technological and philosophical advancement do not make men better. In fact, such things make us more proud, more self-oriented, and therefore more vulnerable to sin. During one of the NASA space flights, I watched in awe as an astronaut maneuvered himself through space with a backpack of rockets. But I couldn't help but think that meanwhile, back on earth, rape, suicide, murder, poverty, and misery continued to escalate. More astounding still is that we selfishly kill our unborn children and call it progress. It is a strange contradiction. It is the ugly scene of self spent on self.

It is significant to note that the strategy of self-centeredness was the centerpiece to Satan's strategy in the attempt to eliminate Christ, the true Messiah, the ultimate threat to the kingdom of Satan. The pattern in the gospel accounts parallels Cain's.

The Pharisees were religious, but had taken authentic Judaism and fashioned it after their own liking. Their religion conveniently served them. It gave them position, prestige, riches, and a great feeling of piety. Pharisaic Judaism was not just slightly out of whack—it was apostate. Jesus came and exposed the whole system, calling for repentance. His offer of God's forgiveness was rejected; it is difficult for a person dedicated to self to admit that there is something wrong with self! The Pharisees became angry with Jesus, and their resultant hatred issued in a desire to extinguish this righteous reminder of their sin (John 15:22–24). They ultimately murdered the Christ.

But three days after the victory of Satan through self-centered leaders, God's theocratic intervention fulfilled the truth of the promise in Genesis 3:15. Christ miraculously rose from the grave as the ultimate stroke against sin, death, and hell!

Christ's resurrection proved the Pharisees wrong and assured them of their judgment. But instead of repenting, they asserted themselves again by joining with their enemies, the Sadduccees. Together, with a sense of false security, they persecuted and killed those who continued to proclaim the truth of the Messiah.

These lessons from our biblical heritage should pierce us to the center of our hearts. We can (and do) fall victim to the same strategy of Satan that worked so well against Cain and against the Pharisees. The lure of self-centeredness is strong. The New Testament refers to self spent on self as the problem of the "flesh," or of our "carnality." God's Word pictures the flesh as something that must be dealt with by devoting ourselves to the reality of our new life in Christ.

Though often disguised in pharisaical robes of piety and religious talk, the self-styled lifestyle is alive and well in many of our hearts. We spend our money, we think, we talk, and we live according to our own desires. We reject the reproof of God's Word and the indwelling Spirit. We discount the prophetic voices that condemn our sins. We dislike believers who model a growing righteousness. If we can find flaws in someone's practice of Christianity, we murder his or her reputation by spreading the news to as many people as possible.

If the problem of selfishness continues unabated, we soon begin to experience the consequences. Feelings of anger, hatred, and alienation grow within us. The church becomes divided. We quickly group with other self-centered Christians to somehow feel better about our flesh-prone activities and attitudes. The Messiah message, the glory of Christ through us, is scandalized. Satan has won the day with the same old strategy of self spent on self.

Watching a self-styled lifestyle unfold is an ugly scene. When confronted with the truth, we should have a renewed motivation to personally implement the triumph of the kingdom of Christ through us. True joy and fulfillment come not by spending self on self, but rather by yielding self to Christ's kingdom.

SELF IN THE KINGDOM OF CHRIST

Several Christian myths about self need to be dealt with before we can chart a course to success. On recognizing the danger of self, many believers sense that self is wrong—a worm, a wretch. Others feel that the yielding of self will result in a humility and meekness that is passive and drab. Some groups of Christians diminish self by downplaying appearance to the extent of perceiving anything that enhances their bodies as being wrong.

Setting these myths aside, the Bible teaches that self actually has a vibrant and exciting role to play in the kingdom of Christ. We should not ignore self; rather, we must be committed to a biblical application of self.

Jesus taught that self has tremendous worth. He said that it is with our selves that we are able to love God totally, to love others, and to love our inner selves. Self is what I have of significance to share with God and others as long as I yield it to God for His service and to others for their benefit. Self is only wrong when it is dedicated to self.

Matthew 20:20–28 describes a clear contrast between those who are committed to *serving* self and those who are committed to *giving* self. James and John self-centeredly desired positions of power and prestige in the coming kingdom. The other ten disciples became enraged—they'd been beaten to the punch! Jesus had twelve "committed" disciples who, at the core of their lives, were committed to the advancement of self. He called them to a new perspective—the perspective of the kingdom of Christ. He taught them that the greatest in His kingdom are those who use self to serve. Servants, those who invest themselves in others, are triumphant in the kingdom.

To dedicate self to the benefit of God and others is a strong defense against sin. That's why Jesus challenges us: "'Love the Lord your God with all your heart and with all your soul and with all your mind.' This is the first and greatest commandment. And the second is like it: 'Love your neighbor as yourself.' All the Law and the Prophets hang on these two commandments" (Matthew 22:37–40).

I have always been enamored with the Old Testament story of Joseph. He was a red-blooded young man away from home and all the positive influences of his childhood. Every single day a beautiful, influential Egyptian woman tried to seduce him. He refused each time. Where did this kind of moral strength come from? According to Joseph, he could not commit such a sin against God or against his responsibility to the woman's husband, his boss (Genesis 39:8–9). In essence, he said that he had committed his self to God and to doing what was right toward others. (We'll examine Joseph's story in more detail in chapter 12.)

I think of Joseph when I hear of men or women who, for the love of another, are willing to deny what is right toward spouse, children, and God. It is easy and convenient to simply pleasure one's self. Yet it is possible to do otherwise. Where are the modern-day Josephs with the courage and commitment to say, "Self is a great treasure. In love, I yield it to God and yield it to others"? Such a commitment results in safety, fulfillment, and success.

The Kingdom Identity of Self

Our victory in the kingdom conflict is actualized by giving self an identity in the kingdom of Christ. At salvation we become new in Him (2 Corinthians 5:17). Essential to that newness is a new identity. Jesus consistently taught and modeled for His followers that our true identity in the kingdom is the identity of a "servant." Since the King by nature is a servant (John 13:4–16; Philippians 2:5–8), so those who are of the kingdom must be servants as well.

A friend of mine was flying first class and overheard the flight attendant ask a rather sophisticated-looking lady across the aisle if she would like a pillow. The lady ignored repeated requests. Finally, the lady's husband leaned over to the flight attendant and said, for all the passengers in the first-class cabin to hear, "My wife does not speak to servants." You can imagine how incensed the flight attendant must have felt! No one likes being called a servant; self wants a better identity than that.

What we don't realize is that servanthood is the best thing that can happen to self. When we serve God unconditionally, we experience the freedom and joy of a clear conscience and the unlimited potential of the Spirit's work through us. When we serve others as Christ served us, we begin to develop meaningful relationships and sense the fulfillment of love, peace, and happiness.

Actualizing the servant self-perspective is the key to triumph in the struggle against Satan. It is also the key to real enjoyment of life. There are three ways that we can serve with self.

First, we should give it *all* as a gift to God (Matthew 22:35–38). After it wholly belongs to Him, He can do with it what He deems best. He is the king, wise and loving, and what He says for my self is what self will do happily and courageously. Resist the tendency to take self back! When you do, give it right back to God again. It's a hot potato in your hand—if you keep it, you're sure to get burned.

Second, God will ask you to take self and give it to the needs of others (Matthew 22:39). All that you have—arms, eyes, feet, hands, thoughts, prayers, money, home, food, cars—are resources for you to share with the needs of others. True servants reject the temptation to focus on their needs alone. They enjoy the ability to sense the needs of others, check their own personal inventory of resources, and then invest themselves in God's name to meet those needs (Philippians 2:3–4).

Third, we must commit to the proper care of self (Matthew 22:39). It is important to have something worthwhile to give to Christ and to others. If we are to be useful servants, we need a spirit that is nourished daily in the Word and prayer, and a body that receives proper food, rest, and exercise.

A commitment to a self-perspective of servanthood will be the beginning of triumph. The kingdom conflict continues, and it makes a difference which side your self is on.

Questions for Your Personal Conflict

1. List all the compound words you can think of that begin with the prefix *self*. (Use a dictionary if you need help.) Which words are usually perceived as negative? Which are positive? How can you maintain a proper perspective of "self" that will allow you to cultivate the positive qualities without developing the negative ones?

2. What are some things you've done recently that you would consider "serving" self?

3. While taking care of yourself is not wrong (within reason), can you think of some opportunities you have to also give your "self" to a worthwhile cause? Can you commit to one or more of these opportunities?

4. In what ways have you observed the self-centeredness of individuals affect a large group in a negative way (family members, a church congregation, and so forth)?

5. Read Luke 18:18–30. How does the issue of self affect the decision of the rich young ruler? What can we learn from him?

5

SEEING PAST THE CAMOUFLAGE
The Battle Against Seduction

Jeff plans to marry Judy next month. He loves her very much. He comes from a Jewish background, but doesn't actually practice the Jewish traditions or attend the religious ceremonies. Judy's Christian beliefs seem a bit strange to him, but she has never pushed them on him. Sure, he has received questioning looks from some of Judy's strongly evangelical family members, but aren't all prospective husbands put under a microscope? After he and Judy get married, they'll work out their religious differences just like all the others: the fact that he wants to go to school in Europe, but Judy's ties to her family are very strong; his reluctance to have kids right away (if at all) while Judy already harps on "when and how many"; and his goal of financial security in light of her service mentality. But he is sure she is the woman for him. Everyone tells them how great they look together.

Judy plans to marry Jeff next month. She loves him very much. Oh, he's still a bit "rough around the edges," but her mom tells her that a good wife can smooth out those rough edges in no time. Jeff is always talking about wild and crazy ideas—going to Europe, making a million dollars by the time he's thirty, and so forth. His absurd dreaming is just one of the things she likes about him. Then there's his Jewish background, but they worship the same God, and isn't He big enough to work out any differences? She knows some of her relatives don't approve of Jeff, and Judy has always tried to do what others expect of her. But she's sure he's the right one for her. Everyone tells them how good they look together.

Suppose you're a pastor, and Judy and Jeff have just asked you to perform their marriage ceremony. Would you have any concerns about uniting these two young and energetic people? What questions would you want to ask them? If they are both obviously in love, and if they look good together, who's to say they shouldn't be allowed to unite and then work out their differences?

It's rarely a simple matter for a pastor to determine who he can, in good conscience, unite in marriage. Almost every young couple is optimistic and naive, and both people are convinced that "love conquers all." Yet it quickly becomes obvious that "love" can have quite a number of definitions. And from my experience, I am convinced that "looking good together" is rarely a criterion for true love.

I've seen far too many marriages where the husband and wife knew ahead of time that they had some significant differences of opinion, yet were expecting that "things will just work out somehow." Anytime two people unite in marriage with a major issue (such as religion) not worked out, problems are bound to arise sooner or later. The marriage weakens little by little as one or both parties pursue their differences rather than what should be a common bond.

I've spoken with many young Christians who were infatuated with nonbelievers, yet preparing to enter the holy bond of marriage. In their minds they knew it would be better to marry a Christian, but in their hearts they were madly in love and seemingly unable to grasp the tremendous implications of their decisions. The vital importance of establishing a godly heritage through their homes falls prey to an emotional attachment. These people unknowingly play into Satan's hand! Marriage between believers and nonbelievers is the very scheme Satan uses to dilute the strength of God's work and to diffuse the power of His Spirit in this generation as well as generations to come.

Of the people I talk to, some I never see again. They disappear into the world of what seems best for themselves. Others struggle through life torn between two loves—their love for God and their love for husband or wife. I sometimes weep with them as they agonize over their children in guilt and confusion. Our mistaken marriage choices become Satan's delight. They are a powerful tool in his arsenal against the kingdom of Christ.

INTERMARRIAGE: AN AGE-OLD TACTIC

After Cain's moral failure and Abel's murder, God sovereignly restored the kingdom potential by providing another son to Adam and Eve. Seth would be a godly line to carry on the promise of the victorious Messiah. It is clear now that Satan's focus of attention will be on the line of Seth because it is the threat to his existence and success.

Genesis 5 traces the family of Seth—the target of Satan's attack. By the time we reach Genesis 6, humanity has become so intolerably wicked that God must judge it with extinction if it doesn't repent. The world has come a long way since men began to call on the name of the Lord (Genesis 4:26).

More significantly, in the light of the kingdom conflict, Satan seems to have cornered God. If God annihilates the human race, then the seed of woman will be snuffed out and Satan is forever clear of the judgment previously pronounced on him (Genesis 3:15). If God permits the evil to escalate, then righteousness and righteous people will be extinct. The victory clearly appears to be Satan's. With Noah as the only righteous person left, time is short and the power of darkness seems to have come to its finest hour yet.

As we come to Genesis 6, we find an unusual observation: "When men began to increase in number on the earth and daughters were born to them, the sons of God saw that the daughters of men were beautiful, and they married any of them they chose" (vv. 1–2). There are two schools of thought in the understanding of this passage. One states that the "sons of God" are the godly line of Seth and the "daughters of men" are the women of the line of Cain from Genesis 4. This view flows nicely with the text and seems to be the natural reading. It is a credible position.

The other approach to the text interprets the "sons of God" to be angels who come to earth and cohabit with women, generating a race that was part angel and part man, making it essentially unre-

deemable and excessively wicked. This view seems to have support
from other texts and may explain the identity of the fallen angels
who are bound in judgment (2 Peter 2:4; Jude 6). Though more
exotic than the first view, it too has credible support. At the core of
both of these views is the problem of *intermarriage*.

Throughout history, one of Satan's most effective schemes has
been intermarriage between godly and ungodly people (Ezra 9:1–2).
Intermarriage reduces loyalty to God and handicaps the efficiency
of Christ through us in this generation and the next. When it is
practiced on a large scale in a given generation, as it often was in
the Old Testament, it leads to quick and certain dilution of righteousness. If the practice continues, a total disintegration of godliness soon takes place in subsequent generations.

It's no wonder that God warned Israel:

> When the Lord your God brings you into the land you are entering
> to possess and drives out before you many nations—the Hittites,
> Girgashites, Amorites, Canaanites, Perizzites, Hivites, and Jebusites,
> seven nations larger and stronger than you—and when the Lord
> your God has delivered them over to you and you have defeated
> them, then you must destroy them totally. Make no treaty with
> them, and show them no mercy. Do not intermarry with them. Do
> not give your daughters to their sons or take their daughters for your
> sons, for they will turn your sons away from following me to serve
> other gods, and the Lord's anger will burn against you and will
> quickly destroy you. (Deuteronomy 7:1–4)

Many of us are troubled by God's Old Testament commands
for the Israelites to totally destroy the cultures they conquered,
including the women and children. However, when viewed in the
context of the kingdom conflict and the high priority of redemption
through the promised Messiah, the issue becomes understandable
and clear. God takes the matter of religious intermarriage seriously.
He knows its great potential for breaking down godliness and establishing a stronghold on a culture.

God planned to use Israel to judge these evil cultures. If Israel
would remain loyal to God by keeping itself removed from the dangerous practices of idolatry and other ungodly cultural customs, the
coming kingdom of Christ would be ensured victory. So God consistently commanded the Israelites not to marry people from those

pagan cultures (Deuteronomy 2:34; 7:1–4; 20:16–18). And consistently, Israel disobeyed (Ezra 9:1–2; Malachi 2:11). As a result, ensuing generations became spiritually weak and idolatrous. Eventually God disciplined the nation by allowing it to be taken captive by foreign nations. In captivity the Israelites became cultural outcasts and therefore able to marry only their own people. During this time, they again learned to lift their faces toward God in repentance.

Intermarriage between the godly and the ungodly has always been a powerful strategy in Satan's conflict against the kingdom of Christ. It still is. Paul reminds us, "Do not be yoked together with unbelievers. For what do righteousness and wickedness have in common? Or what fellowship can light have with darkness?" (2 Corinthians 6:14).

DECEIVED BY OUTER BEAUTY

Since everyone knew intermarriage was prohibited by God, and since the dangers were spelled out clearly, why was it so common? The text quoted earlier gets right to the heart of the matter: "The sons of God saw that the daughters of men were beautiful, and they married any of them they chose" (Genesis 6:2). External beauty was a priority and marriages were based on physical appeal rather than internal, spiritual qualities.

Some time ago a picture in the newspaper caught my eye. A group of guys were sitting around a fountain on the campus of a well-known university. Whenever a girl walked by, each guy would lift up a number from a stack of cards and rate her on a scale of one to ten. It was an unscheduled and demeaning beauty contest, and I'm sure most of the coeds quickly found another way to get to class.

As crude as that kind of treatment seems, many of us do the same thing with a stack of mental cards. We just aren't so obvious about it. We face tremendous pressure to respond to externals. Our society hypes beauty as one of the ultimate marks of acceptance and happiness. Sensuality oozes from well-orchestrated television and magazine advertisements. We are led down the cosmetic path to the temple of outward form and seduced into worshiping there. Consequently, we tend to make life choices based not on the issues of true value, but on externals.

We choose beautiful friends; they enhance our image. We idolize beautiful people who are products of Hollywood studios; they become our heroes. Women quickly learn that outward beauty is a quick and easy way to gain attention, acquire a semblance of security, and develop intimacy with men. Men are encouraged to focus on the external attributes of women as seductive advertisements, pornography, and sexual innuendo saturate our culture. Most significant, marriage choices are often made not on the grounds of true spiritual compatibility, but rather on the outer appeal of physical attractiveness.

As innocent and natural as the appeal of externals may seem, if they become our standard for marriage then we have fallen into the pitfall of Satan's strategy—the scheme that was so effective in Noah's day that all of mankind degenerated beyond the bounds of God's mercy until only one family was left to fulfill the promise of ultimate redemption. How could things have fallen apart so dramatically? How could Satan's kingdom be so overwhelmingly victorious? It was possible because intermarriage between the godly and the ungodly, based on the value system of externals, was the strategy of the world system.

Today's Christians are so inundated with cultural input that we face the same temptation to focus on externals and make choices based on non-Christian standards. We rationalize our decisions with various justifications:

- "She really is a nice person from a good family."
- "I know someday he'll be saved."
- "If I don't marry now, I'll be single for the rest of my life."
- "I can't help it—I'm too much in love."

These statements are all preludes to a smashing victory for Satan as he seeks to dilute the Messiah message through us and weaken generations to come.

A Lot to Lose

As we see from Genesis 6, from the ongoing history of Israel, and sadly from our own experience in this generation, marriage between a godly person and a spiritually uncommitted one yields tragic consequences. Whenever a couple tries to ignore this major difference, they stand to lose much, much more than they gain. Below are some of the potential results Christians should consider before entering marriage alliances with non-Christians.

Guilt

A nagging sense of guilt will haunt the Christian through life. This may result in a defensive spirit that will generate blame and excuses, and may even lead the person away from God's people. Reminders will be everywhere. Families who are complete in Christ will be a continuing source of remembrance for the person's rebellion against God and His Word. The thought of "what might have been" will lead to further guilt and despair.

Loss of Compatibility

Much of the joy in life comes from compatibility—finding an ever-deepening sense of belonging. Full, wholesome relationships with both God and others are primary sources of fulfillment. Marriage to someone who doesn't share one's faith shortchanges the fullness of that joy. If we adjust to the mind-set, lifestyle, emotions, and desires of the unsaved partner, we lose our compatibility with God. If we remain loyally committed to the principles and values of the kingdom of Christ, then there will be a loss of compatibility with the unsaved partner (2 Corinthians 5:17). This automatically reduces the fulfillment factor of life regardless of which choice we make. It also provides the ground for bitterness, anger, and resentment either toward God, a partner, or others whom we may wish to blame for our unhappiness.

Hindered Effectiveness

Effective ministry within the body of Christ is often minimized because an unsaved spouse is rarely empathetic to the time and attention that is necessary to prepare for and invest in the needs of other believers.

Social Stress

With differing interests, the social life of couples often suffers as both partners go their individual ways, stifling the joy of oneness that should exist in marriage.

Children Jeopardized

Unfortunately, the consequences of spiritually mixed marriages often ripple into the next generation. Instead of having a unified structure of biblical teaching and morality, children discover the option of an alternative lifestyle. This threatens to diminish their spiritual commitment and vibrancy. Children are also provided with a precedent to marry outside their faith if they so choose. This was exactly what happened to the line of Seth in Genesis 6 and to the nation of Israel in subsequent history. The sins of the fathers are visited upon the third and fourth generation (Deuteronomy 5:9).

VALUES AT STAKE

In Genesis 5 and 6 the value of a solid spiritual heritage and the development of a strong God-centered family was, over the course of time, traded away for self-fulfillment in a world that focused on external qualities. Since we live in a similar cultural environment today, it is our responsibility to fortify the value of Christ-centered homes so that the Messiah message might be strong in our generation and the generations to come.

Where does triumph begin in the kingdom conflict? It begins with parental influence and is fortified by the Christian community at large. Parents must begin early to instill in their children some guidelines for selecting a mate.

Abraham's selection of a life partner for Isaac is a classic example of parental commitment to a strong marriage in the next generation (Genesis 24). Though we as parents don't personally select our children's partners, we can be committed to the same ideals and pass them on to our children. Here are a few principles we can start with.

Principle 1: *Never consider marrying anyone outside the scope of your spiritual heritage* (Genesis 24:3–4).

Abraham was firm about not having Isaac marry a Canaanite girl. He made his servant swear to follow this plan. The servant made a firm commitment, which involved his taking a long journey into uncertain territory. Yet his commitment to Abraham and Isaac turned out to be well worth the effort.

Principle 2: *Never spiritually backtrack for marriage* (Genesis 24:5–6).

The servant proposed that Isaac go back to Abraham's homeland and get married there. Surely the servant wondered what girl in her right mind would return with him to marry Isaac—sight unseen. But Abraham recognized that God had led him to the Promised Land for a purpose and was unwilling to let his son backtrack on God's plan for the sake of marriage. Marriage should never be a reason to compromise the development of God's best in and through us. The right partner will complement God's best in us— not compete against it!

Unfortunately, some parents tend to put tremendous pressure on their children to get married. From the time the kids are small until they reach their late twenties, Mom and Dad verbally and nonverbally communicate that marriage is the most important thing in the world and that singleness is a plague. Nothing could be further from the truth. In spite of any desires we have to see our children get married, we need to let them know with certainty that knowing and following God's will for them is the highest value in life.

As a Bible college student, Janet had given her life to God and was preparing to devote herself to world missions. Then she fell in love and decided to marry a promising young businessman. He came from a good family, but he was not a Christian. Now, years later, Janet is often troubled with guilt, bitterness, and depression. She struggles with the fact that she married against God's will, and her inner conflict has plagued her, her home, and her children for years.

Principle 3: *Maintain an unflinching trust in God* (Genesis 24:7–8).

We shouldn't feel that it is up to us to "make things happen" when it comes to finding marriage partners. A recognition of God's supernatural participation and an unflinching trust in His provision in His time is essential to the process. God is able to provide the right person as a life partner within the scope of His revealed will.

Principle 4: *Make a commitment to these principles before you begin searching for a partner* (Genesis 24:9).

An obedient commitment to discover and obey the will of God for marriage must be made early—even in adolescence, before dating begins. Parents, creatively nurture your children in this mind-set. Spend time with them, both playing and teaching. Don't be threatened or surprised by their ideas or weird statements. Teach them the importance of a godly heritage by using both Scripture and personal experience. Be loving, patient, and firm. Don't give ground on this important matter.

Principle 5: *Go where the fishing's good* (Genesis 24:10–11).

Abraham's servant traveled back to where there were eligible women within the scope of his covenant with Abraham. If you want to fall in love with people of a compatible spiritual heritage, then socialize accordingly. Friendships and relationships can begin in church youth groups or singles groups, Christian colleges, or campus groups that feature a commitment to Christ and discipleship. People who meet and make commitments to God can then grow closer to each other while growing closer to Him as well.

Principle 6: *Pray* (Genesis 24:12–14).

Abraham's servant prayed that God would make him successful in his search. Prayer has significant power. A commitment by parents to pray for a child's life partner, and then by the child to pray for his or her life partner, will lead to a deepening determination to put these principles into practice.

Principle 7: *Ask God for discernment* (Genesis 24:15–21).

Choosing someone who is "outwardly" a believer can often prove to be rather disappointing. Often, a dating partner will put on a great facade of spirituality which is shed the moment the wedding bells stop ringing. God provides wisdom to help us "see through" the false pretenses of other people. The ability to discern positive character traits should be a primary goal in the process of choosing a mate.

First, try to discern why you are interested in pursuing a relationship with a given partner. Awareness of the wrong motives for continuing a relationship is just as important as knowing what is involved in a right relationship. Some such wrong motives that drive people to pursue improper relationships include: security and social acceptance, pressure from parents and peers, sexual activity followed by a sense of moral obligation, the prospect of riches and success, or a desire to help a rebellious, immature, or irresponsible partner. If a relationship is continued for reasons like these, disaster is inevitable. Take courage and renounce any relationships that exist for the wrong reasons. Instead, build relationships on a solid spiritual foundation and seek partners who exhibit positive character traits.

QUALITIES TO LOOK FOR

It is instructive to note the basis for Abraham's servant's interest in Rebekah. The qualities she had developed set a standard for anyone looking for a meaningful marriage partner today.

Neat Appearance (Genesis 24:16)

We all will not win beauty contests, but we all can do the best with what we have. Appropriate clothing with colors and styles that reflect our personality is important. Hair and grooming are clues to our sense of self-worth and decency. Our countenance—eyes, smile, and facial expressions—reflects what's happening on the inside. These kinds of external signals do serve as barometers of internal values.

Moral Purity (Genesis 24:16)

The ability to maintain moral priorities when facing strong inner desire and cultural pressure is a high mark of personal strength and commitment to Christ. Even those who have previously failed in this area can restore their strength of commitment to high values in the area of sexuality.

Respect for Authority (Genesis 24:18)

It was Rebekah's cultural custom to speak to a man with respect. Though she had never seen Abraham's servant before, Rebekah addressed him as "lord." The ability to relate properly and interact respectfully with others is a key in any relationship. People who have a spirit of rebellion against parents, school officials, employers, or even spiritual leaders are likely to carry that attitude into their relationships with their marriage partners.

Hospitality (Genesis 24:17–18)

What is more important in a home than a sense of openness and warmth? Selfish people make difficult marriage partners. The expression of genuine interest in others is a major plus in partnership and a good reflection of spiritual maturity.

Willingness to Go the Extra Mile (Genesis 24:19–20)

Did you ever give a camel a drink? How about ten camels? Rebekah "volunteered" to not only give the servant a drink, but to water his camels as well. That meant walking down into the well and bringing up water for them—again and again. Good relationships are created by people who are willing to stretch for each other.

Abraham's servant was impressed. He discovered in Rebekah a woman of true inner beauty. In a world that measured by external factors, he found a believer who was committed to the strength of the Messiah message. We, too, need to seek out life partners who not only provide lip service to Christ's kingdom, but who also demonstrate a good measure of inner spiritual strength as well.

Foundational to these measures of inner beauty is the essential quality of love. Successful love in marriage is more than flowers, candy, sensual fulfillment, and feeling good about each other. After Isaac and Rebekah met and got married, we discover that Isaac "loved" Rebekah (Genesis 24:67). The importance of Christlike love in a marriage relationship is underscored in the New Testament (Ephesians 5:25; Titus 2:3–4). Christ's love is accepting, unconditional, and primarily interested in meeting someone else's needs.

When dating, it is crucial to discern if your dates are in the relationship for themselves or if they really care about *your* needs and interests. What do they talk about? Where do they take you? Do they encourage you to break your moral commitments to Christ, inflicting you with guilt and fear and leading you away from God's best?

And what are *you* looking for in the relationship? Are you committed to discerning the needs of those you date and meeting their needs even if it means personal sacrifice?

THE CHURCH'S RESPONSIBILITY

The church must reinforce values through teaching and maintaining an emphasis on the value of godly homes. This can be done in several ways:

- Provide good social climates where single Christians can meet other Christians.
- Fill those social settings with creative teaching about relationships that lead to solid commitments.
- Refuse to sanction or perform marriages that violate God's serious warnings about intermarriage.
- Feature singleness as a viable, God-ordained, and blessed lifestyle. Integrate and elevate the singles into the mainstream of the church family.
- Encourage young people to find their primary social life in groups that share a mutual commitment to Christ.
- Place high value on inner strength and character by recognizing and affirming such qualities through genuine compliments and clear teaching. Downplay external factors as a measure of status and prestige. Value them only as a reflection of what the person is like on the inside.
- Renounce pornography and the subtle forms of immorality that take our focus off of Christian values and lead us into the shallow, destructive influence of externals alone.
- Provide resources (books, retreats, seminars, tapes) to help those who are engaged and those who are already married to establish godly patterns in their homes.

THE SPIRITUAL POWER OF HERITAGE

Few things are more powerful in the hand of God than a spiritually solid family atmosphere. Good homes become great heritages that can last for generations. One of the great Bible teachers of this generation is a fifth-generation pastor. Another leading family counselor speaks of a grandfather who prayed every day for the strength and success of his children and grandchildren—even before they were born.

I currently work at Moody Bible Institute, a Christian college in downtown Chicago that has had a strong ministry through many generations. It is a delight to interact with students and spiritual leaders whose heritage reaches back to people who were connected with the Institute years ago. In many cases, the torch has been handed down from godly home to godly home.

E. H. Erikson wrote, "The strength of the generations . . . depends on the process by which the youths of two sexes find their respective identities, fuse them in love or marriage, revitalize their respective traditions, and together create and 'bring up' the next generation." But as we have seen in Genesis 6, the generations of that period were not revitalizing their godly traditions. Rather, the world had become so decadent through intermarriage that God had to theocratically intervene to save the Messiah seed. The only righteous man, Noah, would be preserved to maintain the kingdom of Christ and ensure its victory. God would begin again.

God's theocratic hand broke open the moist canopy of the sky and the waters of the deep, and He purified the world with the Flood. To sovereignly guarantee that evil would never accumulate again in like manner, God shortened the life span of mankind (Genesis 5; 6:3; 11:10–26) and asked them not to congregate, but to spread out and "fill" the earth (9:1). This command would set the stage for Satan's next attack on the Genesis 3:15 promise. But for now the victory of Christ had been guaranteed, not by the righteous choices of men, but by the intervening hand of God.

Questions for Your Personal Conflict

1. Can you recall a situation where you were led astray (or tempted to do so) by a "pretty face"? How would you handle the situation differently if you had it to do over again?

2. Think of someone close to you who has recently been through a divorce. What would you say was the major reason that led to the breakup? In retrospect, do you think the divorce could have been avoided? How?

3. Can you think of a marriage that you questioned at first, yet that worked out quite well? If so, what would you say made it work?

4. Read the Noah account in Genesis 6–9. What can we learn from Noah about leading a righteous life when so many others around us are being seduced by outer beauty?

5. Can you think of a young person who might benefit from your past experience and/or advice regarding dating and marriage? If so, try to schedule a time for an informal discussion sometime soon. (Perhaps you can include the story of Isaac and Rebekah and the principles from this chapter.) You might even consider getting something started on a churchwide level as well.

6

TONGUE-TIED AT THE TOWER
The Battle Against Pride

I have often wished I could go back in history to watch significant events unfold. If I had a time machine, I would push the button to return to the Tower of Babel. Imagine being there and watching the people feverishly building that great city with its tower that reached high into the sky. From his scaffold Fred the bricklayer calls to Sam for more bricks. But Sam can't believe what he's hearing! He turns to a buddy and laughs that Fred's "been in the sun too long," and to his amazement, his buddy blurts out some pre-Chinese response. You can be sure it was the quickest any building project has been shut down in history. I doubt if the union steward was even able to file a grievance.

When God decides to ensure the success of His plan, He has options we've never dreamed of. That's exactly why human language was confused at Babel. Yet the Babel story is far more than the history of modern languages. Its meaning goes beyond a judgment on people who wanted to build a tower into heaven. The confusion of tongues in Genesis 11 was no less than God's hand of theocratic intervention to save the Messiah seed from extinction at the hand of Satan's kingdom.

Unlike the provision of Seth when the theocratic kingdom exercised its authority *after* there was no one left to carry the Messiah promise, and, unlike the theocratic intervention of the

Flood *just in the nick of time* to save the one remaining righteous family, this rescue mission was a preventative stroke by God to abort an attack of Satan's domain *before* it got off the ground (quite literally).

What I remember as a child in Sunday school is that God was upset that men would build a tower as high as heaven, trying to intrude into His territory. But if that's all that was happening at Babel, I find little relevance in this bit of history for us today. Yet much to the surprise of my childhood notions, there is a much greater significance to this account. It is a story with much relevance. What happened at Babel is an up-to-date pattern of behavior that Satan still masterfully uses to choke out the Messiah message.

Satan's Attack at Babel

Genesis 9–11 records the history of Noah's family. Chapter 10 provides the genealogies of Noah's three sons with the editorial comment at the end of each section that they were divided according to "their clans and languages, in their territories and nations." Chapter 11 gives us the reason that these divisions took place.

By their own testimony, the people's plan to build Babel meant three things (11:4). First, they would *build a city* in which they would construct a tower that would reach far into the heavens, or literally, the sky.

Second, through the building of this city and tower they would make *a name for themselves*. This desire to make a name for themselves is significant. In the context of the biblical meaning of the word *name* is the intent that they wanted to become independent from God and glorify themselves. The commentary on Seth's generation was that "men began to call on the name of the Lord" (4:26). At that time mankind was submissive to Him and recognized His place of authority over them. But now, if they had their way, people would be their own lords and make a name for themselves. They would live for their own glory.

This craving for independence from God comes to light in their third intention, which was *not to be scattered abroad upon the face of the earth*. To understand the relevance of their intention, we must recall God's will for them as expressed in Genesis 9:1. After the Flood, the people were told to "fill the earth." This was not simply a command to have children, but to spread out and inhabit the entire world. If people grouped together, with one language and one purpose, and built a city as Cain did, then wickedness would have a greater potential to escalate unchecked (11:6). Satan would have all of humanity in one place with one language where his lie could be communicated and Christ's kingdom defeated.

THE URBAN PROBLEM

A city is a monument to man and his glory. In the city are few reminders of God. The lights blur the glory of God in the nighttime sky and the smoggy air diffuses the beauty of the clean, warm sun. Even the few trees we plant on our bustling sidewalks struggle to make it from season to season.

Like the people at Babel, we too have our "towers." Skyscrapers stand as monuments to our genius. They are our glory. The city is the marketplace of materialism and offers us waters from the wells of pride, self-sufficiency, and sensuous living. This is not to say that the country is inherently more moral than the city. But the city makes it easier to lose an awareness of God while becoming more independent from Him, more self-sufficient, and more proud of our own accomplishments. In the urban environment, self-glory and independence from God can thrive.

Those who live off the land outside the confines of the city must depend on God for rain, sun, and seasons. Just as the glory of God in Creation reminds them of His presence, so the harvest reminds them of His provision. Whether they accept this perspective does not alter the reality that it is a truth they must personally deal with. We are not better at the core when we live in the country, but our sinfulness has fewer restraints in the city.

The city's potential for escalating evil is God's concern, and justly so. Think of the first city. It was technologically advanced, yet greatly sinful (Genesis 4:17–24). This may very well have been the reason God told people to "fill the earth," and why the end result of God's intervention was scattering them across the face of the earth.

THE LANGUAGE PROBLEM

The grouping of people with one language was also a concern of God (Genesis 11:5–6). Scripture makes it clear that Satan's system of operation is based on a lie (3:16; John 8:42–47). The decision to become their own people apart from God and have a common language would provide Satan's kingdom the ideal opportunity to spread lies about God and to integrate those falsehoods into the people's daily lives.

The more extensive our communication becomes (i.e., TV, radio, film, magazines, books, satellites, education), the more Satan's lie entangles our minds and makes us vulnerable to sin, thus diminishing the Messiah message through us. All the major means of communication today are dominated by the godless philosophies of Satan's domain. Advertisements, television entertainment, documentaries, books, and magazine articles can be tools of Satan's kingdom to sabotage our network of information with his lies about life, relationships, and material goods. And with the ease of translation into other languages, the lies are quickly transmitted to other geographic locations and cultures. Such was God's concern at Babel.

Today, more than ever, we need to be alert to the lies of Satan and able to differentiate them from God's truth. With the recent introduction of the "World Wide Web" on the internet, we are closer than we have ever been to having a common language among all the people of the earth, and, like Babel, mankind is taking great pride in his own accomplishments.

The internet system is promoted with promises of accessing libraries, museums, and unlimited information anywhere in the world—all from the computer terminal in your den. The focus has been on what we are able to learn and the various ways we can better ourselves. Yet in spite of all the potential advantages, one of the first realities of the system has been the availability of pornography and computer sex made available to any user—young children included. The "common language" of the information superhighway promises great things, and there is certainly nothing inherently wrong with it. But in the hands of ungodly people and forces, it is a tool that can manipulate the thinking of unwary people and has the potential for damage as well as good.

The time and setting at Babel were ripe for another destructive attack by the kingdom of Satan against humanity, the designed channel of the Messiah. The people would be gods to themselves; their city and its tower would be their glory. Their one language would be the channel of Satan's lie. By refusing to obey God's command to "fill the earth," mankind again chose not to be under God's dominion. The confusion of tongues and resultant scattering was God's theocratic option that protected His promise and thwarted Satan's assault.

Satan attempted to use mankind's desire for self-glorifying independence against the Messiah Himself. Soon after Jesus' birth, the wise men informed Herod that the King of the Jews had been born (Matthew 2:11–18). But at that time Herod considered *himself* the king of the Jews. His "city" was Israel. His "tower" was his position, his claim to fame. In a vicious attack of the kingdom of Satan on the Messiah, Herod ordered all Jewish boys two years and under to be killed. Herod did everything in his power to protect his own name and his own glory, even at the expense of God's will and God's plan. Yet God theocratically intervened with an angelic warning, and the kingdom of Christ remained safe.

WHOSE GLORY?

The strategy Satan used at the Tower of Babel still has a profound relevance for us. We are all city builders by nature. We build our personal cities of wealth, fame, and success—cities with "towers" of cars, wardrobes, oversized egos, and anything else that elevates our own glory. Seeking to make a name for ourselves instead of for Him, we reject His lordship and demand independence from His will.

When we glorify self, we detach ourselves from His purpose for us. Just as God commanded Noah's family to scatter, we too have a distinct commission. Our commission is to bring glory not to ourselves, but rather to God's name (1 Corinthians 6:19–20; 10:31; 2 Corinthians 3:18; Romans 8:29). As the Westminster Catechism says, "The chief end of man is to glorify God and enjoy Him forever."

Self-glorified independence leads to certain disobedience.

When pursuing cities of wealth and the accumulation of things, we may reject the biblical guidelines for stewardship of our finances. When we glorify our egos by boasting, we deny the truth that all we are and all we have is because of God. In attempting to build the "tower" of corporate mobility, we may sever ourselves from the integrity of honesty and biblical ethics. To glorify our bodies, we may pay the spiritual price of immodesty or moral failure. At the very essence of self-glorification is the denial of our true identity as servants. Self-glory is rooted in pride. As it was with the descendants of Noah, self-glory and independence from God go hand in hand.

If we commit ourselves to self-glory, we too become vulnerable for defeat as soldiers in Christ's kingdom. If we hope to be victorious, it is imperative that we renew our sense of purpose, God's purpose. We need to be clear about what it is that God wants us to do.

The world has a clear definition of purpose. Most people can tell you in which general direction they are headed—whether it be the materialist committed to happiness through the accumulation of possessions, the hedonist whose motto is to eat, drink, and be merry, the narcissist who exists for the fulfillment of self, or the secular humanist who lives with no God, but rather the god of himself and his community.

Many believers lack such a degree of purpose in their lives. We live like meandering streams nudged in one direction, then another, by the influences of the world. Perhaps you can identify with the bumper sticker that says, "Don't follow me, I'm lost." Better yet, you may feel like Charlie Brown. On a cruise, Charlie and Lucy each grab a deck chair. Lucy unfolds her chair, faces it forward, and says, "Charlie Brown, some people live life like this, looking at all that is ahead. Some set their chairs to look toward where they are, and others set their chairs to look toward all that is behind." The last frame of the cartoon shows Charlie with a dejected look, clutching his deck chair, saying, "Lucy, I can't even get my chair unfolded."

GOD'S GLORY

The conquering Christian lets the Word of God unfold the deck chair of his life and permits God to position it in the divinely appointed direction. God never intended for us to live without a clear sense of direction and purpose. His purpose for us is unmistakable, and when we are committed to Him, He fortifies us against the destructive self-glorifying independence of the world system. God's fundamental purpose for us is that we should glorify Him. That's why He has redeemed us (1 Corinthians 6:19–20). Glorifying God is to be our all-pervading reason for being (10:31) and the evidence of our spiritual maturity (2 Corinthians 3:18).

What does it mean to glorify God? Let's begin with an understanding of God's glory. First, God's glory is the sum total of all that He is. It is His love, grace, mercy, sovereignty, honesty, holiness, justice, righteousness—the entirety of His being. Second, God's glory is something He has chosen to reveal through specially assigned channels. The psalmist said, "The heavens declare the glory of God" (Psalm 19:1). A clear starlit night reveals God's unlimited power, constancy, and awesome design. The seen things of nature are a reflection of the unseen qualities of God (Romans 1:20).

God chose the nation Israel as a channel of His glory. At the Red Sea, we see through Israel that God is a faithful deliverer. When He provides them with manna in the wilderness, we see that God is a supplier of mankind's needs. At Jericho, we see that God reaches down to save us from the problem of sin. Jesus Christ revealed the glory of God (John 1:14). The Bible, at its very core, is the express revelation of what God is.

It excites me to realize that God has redeemed me to join this select group of special channels of His revelation. It is through believers that God shows His character and likeness. This is essentially what it means to glorify God. God is glorified when His abundant love, mercy, justice, and righteousness are revealed through my personal encounters. He is glorified when I tactfully give Him the credit for all He has done and provided, and for all that He is.

OUR CAPACITY TO GLORIFY GOD

From the beginning, we were intended to be image-bearers for God, reflections of His likeness (Genesis 1:26–27). Being created in His image means that just as God has a will, emotions, and personality, so also mankind would be created with a will, emotions, and personality. God's will, emotions, and personality were to flow down through His created people so that an invisible God could reveal what He was like.

The Fall of man (Genesis 3) realigned our nature to reflect the will, emotions, and personality of Satan and his system. Redemption was God's way of restoring us to our original purpose (1 Corinthians 6:19–20). His indwelling Spirit became the internal dynamic that would lead and teach us for the purpose of glorifying Him (John 16:12–15). This divine purpose requires that I commit to align myself with God by submitting my will to His will, and to submit my emotions and character to the work of the Spirit that I might reflect His character. But alignment is not easy.

One day while driving home I hit a major pothole. I thought my car was going to disassemble right on the spot. Stepping out of the car at home, I heard a hissing sound. As I checked the tire, I noticed it was becoming flatter by the second and that the hubcap was gone. After fixing the tire, I hurried back to the pothole to retrieve my hubcap. Walking along the road at that fateful spot, I found three hubcaps. I took the one I thought was mine and drove home, only to discover that it didn't fit. So back to the pothole I went, this time checking both sides of the road. I found nine hubcaps before I located the right one. The pothole had damaged my car's original glory and thrown it out of alignment. And from all indications, it had done the same to many others as well.

Satan's attempts to influence our will, emotions, and personality are potholes in the street of our existence. When we have a direct encounter with one of them, we tend to jar our spiritual alignment with God and cease to reflect His glory. We disable our ability to be what God wants us to be.

As we realign ourselves with God's will, emotions, and character, we must be committed to two important dynamics of God's glory through us. We are to honor God, and we are to do so through our bodies, the totality of our being (1 Corinthians 6:20).

WHERE CREDIT IS DUE

We must remember that as God's glory becomes evident in us, we must tactfully give Him the credit. God takes it seriously when we take credit for His glory. Moses was denied entrance to the Promised Land because he claimed that he and Aaron would provide water from a rock. In reality, the water was God's provision (Numbers 20:7–12). Nebuchadnezzar was banished to the field as a wild beast because he claimed the glory for his kingdom (Daniel 4:30–37). Herod was struck dead for accepting praise as a god (Acts 12:21–23). As we experience the glory of God through us, we must be willing to give credit where credit is due.

One night Martie and the children came home from the mall bearing sacks of new clothes for the summer. A style show ensued and excitement was running high. I began to feel good about how I had earned the money to provide for my family. What a great father! While I was patting myself on the back and secretly hoping that someone would start singing my praises, the Lord reminded me that He is our ultimate provider. My feelings of pride turned to thankfulness. My false sense of glory turned to a spirit of praise to the glory of God. As I tucked the children into bed, I asked them if they knew where the clothes had come from. They each said that the Lord had provided them. My youngest said, "God gave you the job that gave us the money to buy our clothes." Good answer! We all prayed with thanksgiving for His provision, and God got the credit He deserved.

I am convinced that when God trusts us to glorify Him, He will begin to work in special ways through us. President Reagan kept a sign on his desk that read, "There is no limit to what a man can do if he doesn't care who gets the credit." Biblically, there is no limit to what God can do through us if we are willing to give Him the credit. That's what it means to glorify His name.

BODY LANGUAGE

Yet glorifying God is to be more than lip service. It is to be body language (1 Corinthians 6:20), not just words. This phase of commitment is especially helpful when we think of the potholes of immorality, negative habits, and even the challenge of good manners. While it is relatively easy to tell people what God is like, it is even more significant to *show* them with our actions.

I remember a conversation with a woman whose husband had

just died. She told me she knew that God was good and wise and that He never made mistakes. She said that's what many people had recently affirmed to her about God. Yet she confessed, quite candidly, that what she knew in her head was not how she felt in her heart. Those words about God, though meant to comfort her, didn't touch her hurt. Her husband had been suddenly and tragically snatched from her, and she was having a terrible struggle with the emptiness inside. She went on to tell me that the previous Sunday a friend had walked up to her and said nothing at all. That friend simply put her arms around the woman and held her tight. I'll never forget her words. She said, "It was like the arms of God around my life!"

This woman's friend knew what it meant to glorify God in her body. In the despair of the woman's situation, the friend did just what God would have done.

It was unusual for my whole family to be invited to a banquet, and even more unusual that we were all seated at the raised speaker's table. Beside me was the leader of the whole affair, whose name tag proudly announced him to be "John." Between the meal and the program, my son Matt came behind the chairs and asked to sit on my lap. I picked him up and landed him right where he wanted to be. Well, as soon as Matt hit my lap, he threw out his hand in friendship toward this man he had never met before, read the name tag, and confidently proclaimed, "Hi, John."

Matt knew that when we go to restaurants, I usually read the server's name tag and call him or her by name—much to the consternation and embarrassment of my children. But he didn't have to tell John, "Excuse me, sir, let me tell you what my dad is like. When he meets someone he reads his name tag and calls him by name." Not on your life! John could tell from Matt's actions what kind of person I was because Matt's a chip off the old block!

We are to be chips off the divine block. With all of our minds, wills, and personalities, we are to be the express image of our Father and bring glory to His name. We become conquerors for the kingdom of Christ by rejecting self-glorifying independence from God and committing ourselves to a submissive alignment with Him. Christ's kingdom must be our city, His name must be our glory, and His will our supreme joy.

Our prayer should flow with the words of Frances Havergal:

Take my life, and let it be consecrated, Lord, to Thee;
Take my hands, and let them move at the impulse of Thy love.
Take my feet, and let them be swift and beautiful for Thee;
Take my voice, and let me sing always, only, for my King.
Take my lips, and let them be filled with messages for Thee;
Take my silver and my gold, not a mite would I withhold.
Take my love, my God, I pour at Thy feet its treasure store;
Take myself and I will be ever, only, all for Thee.

Questions for Your Personal Conflict

1. The Tower of Babel was an attempt to display self-ability and self-glory while disregarding God's clear commands and direction. Can you think of modern-day equivalents of grand self-glorification? How about less extreme examples?

2. Do you find it easier to experience God's presence in city or country settings? Why? What specific things can you do to ensure an ongoing relationship with God when you find yourself away from your preferred location?

3. It doesn't take speaking different languages to cause a breakdown in communications. What are some potential communication problems Christians should be aware of if they wish to work well together (and stay within the will of God)?

4. As worldwide communication improves, what potential benefits can you envision? What potential problems?

5. Read Philippians 2:1–11. What are some specific steps you can take to develop unity and cooperation with others without also developing an attitude of self-glory (like the people at the Tower of Babel)?

1

FAITH IN MOTION
The Battle Against Spiritual Stagnation

Suppose it's time for a vacation. You debate on where to go and what to do, when you recall a marvelous time you had as a kid at Hidden Lake, a resort tucked away among some of the most beautiful woods you've ever seen. The water had been cobalt blue, reflecting the majesty of the sky and the hills that surrounded it. Your family had spent a week fishing, skiing, swimming, and hiking in bare feet through the beautiful sand. With hardly a second thought, you decide it's time to take your own family to such a vacation wonderland.

But as the minivan arrives at your destination, you notice that the "Hidden Lake" signs have been replaced with signs reading "Stagnant Pond." Upon inquiry, you discover the source that had previously fed the lake has dried up and the water in the lake has become stagnant. The resort still exists, but you can't understand why. The wonderful, fresh smells you recall have become pungent almost to the point of being toxic. The sand is no longer clean and white, but rather greenish and slimy. The water that had been so pure now has a layer of scum across its surface. All the fish have died, but the locals tell you it's now a good place to find frogs—if you don't mind the billions of mosquitoes breeding in the stagnant water. You begin to suspect that the skiing and swimming might not be as enjoyable this trip.

If we are not careful, our spiritual lives tend to become like stagnant ponds. They start out with the freshness and newness that only God can provide, but inactivity leads to stagnation. And if we are satisfied with stagnation, we can become a feeding ground for dozens of nuisances and the playground for the frogs of the world.

God wants a rushing river—a powerful force going somewhere for Him. His kingdom is mobile and requires a moving army. It demands obedient soldiers who will step out for Him in routine faithfulness. It means marching to the beat of His drum. It means guarding against the propensity to step out on God (as Jonah did) or step *ahead* of God or lag *behind* Him. It is being committed to God as our pacesetter. Regardless.

Kingdom people are meant to be people in process—people continually growing and becoming more like Christ. This process is a lifelong development of our spiritual potential, yet it takes place one step at a time. It's a slow yet significant stretch.

It was one step at a time for Abraham. For him, leaving his home in Ur of the Chaldeans was the first step into the unknown and the beginning of a process that would unfold far beyond the parameters of his lifetime. He would die with promises unfulfilled. God's kingdom needed his commitment then for events that wouldn't take place until generations—even centuries—later.

The refreshing appeal of Genesis 12 is that Abraham was a smashing success! I rejoice in the victory accounts in Scripture. They stimulate me. They prove to me what is possible when people are bold enough to obey God in spite of their own fears and concerns. Though I see that success seldom comes easily, I am encouraged to play my part in the victory of Christ over the dominion of Satan.

A THREE-DIMENSIONAL PROCESS

God sovereignly chose Abraham and Sarah to become stewards of the promised victory through Christ (Genesis 12:1–3). He made great promises to them and asked them for their lives through which He would accomplish His purposes. Their assignment? Leave home and head for a place that God would show them (Genesis 12:1; Hebrews 11:8). Abraham obeyed. He stepped out with God, became mobile, and entered the process. It was a process that demanded three things from Abraham.

First, the process demanded *obedience*, a submitted will (Hebrews 11:8). There is essentially one key principle to spiritual mobility: God is the boss and can unconditionally call the shots in our lives.

At every crossroad—financial, family, thought-life, relationships, or activities—we must take gladly the path of "not my will, but yours be done" (Luke 22:42). As the old country preacher used to say, "God says it; I believe it; that settles it!" Stubbornness stagnates us, but submission stimulates God in us.

Second, Abraham's process demanded *persistence*. Victory is not assured at the altar of commitment. It is won in the persistence of our hearts not to flinch from our resolve to obey. Abraham followed God's road map into the new land without looking back (Hebrews 11:9, 15–16). He stayed in the groove of God's process in his life. The process demands determination over the long haul, often without seeing any results.

The important things in life demand persistence: parenting, a quiet time with God, pastoring, Sunday school teaching, resisting the devil, and breaking the bondage of bad habits. Persistence allows us to be people in process for Christ rather than giving up the first time things get difficult or inconvenient.

Third, the process involved *productivity*. Twenty-five years after obeying God and leaving their home country, Abraham and Sarah gave birth to Isaac, the promised son of the messianic line (Hebrews 11:11–12). Persistent obedience is not a dead-end street. God will produce His plan through us in His time and His way, as long as we remain faithful. Productivity is the ultimate purpose of the process. John captured the essence of this thought when he recorded Christ's words:

> I am the vine; you are the branches. If a man remains in me and I in him, he will bear much fruit; apart from me you can do nothing. If anyone does not remain in me, he is like a branch that is thrown away and withers; such branches are picked up, thrown into the fire and burned. If you remain in me and my words remain in you, ask whatever you wish, and it will be given you. This is to my Father's glory, that you bear much fruit, showing yourselves to be my disciples. (John 15:5–8)

I'm a gardener at heart. Each spring I used to plant rows of peas, carrots, peppers, tomatoes, and a few exotic types of vegetables. The joy of the gardening process was picking and eating the crisp, fresh, juicy fruit of my labor. Before that could happen, though, a process of obedience and persistence was necessary. I had to submit to the laws of nature. I couldn't plant too late or too early. Seeds could not be too deep, too shallow, or too close together. Then came the difficult stretch of persisting in weeding, watering, pruning, thinning—a lot of work with no immediate reward. But, in season, the payoff arrived. Then the pain was worth the gain.

Our friends, missionaries in Mexico, labored with a tribe of Indians for many years. They patiently built relationships with the nationals, meticulously translated the Scriptures, and waited for God to work. Nothing happened. Year after year, furlough after furlough, their reports were only of hope, not of happening. Many missionaries would have given up, but Phil and Mary were process people. They persisted in their obedience to God and committed the process to Him. In time, God's time, the tribe exploded spiritually. The native people began turning to Christ in great numbers, and today a solid church thrives for God's glory because two of God's people placed themselves in process and persistently obeyed until they saw productivity.

Stepping out with God is described in Paul's prayer for the Colossian believers:

> For this reason, since the day we heard about you, we have not stopped praying for you and asking God to fill you with the knowledge of his will through all spiritual wisdom and understanding. And we pray this in order that you may live a life worthy of the Lord and may please him in every way: bearing fruit in every good work, growing in the knowledge of God, being strengthened with all power according to his glorious might so that you may have great endurance and patience. (Colossians 1:9–11)

Hebrews 11:8 states that Abraham, "when called to go to a place he would later receive as his inheritance, obeyed and went, even though he did not know where he was going." For Abraham, obedience meant a step into the unknown with no details about where or when. I think of all the "what ifs" that must have raced through his mind. *What if this is only a figment of my imagination?*

What if I'm not happy? What if there is danger out there? What if God is really not a good God? What if my friends criticize and reject me?

Think of how difficult it is to obey when God asks you to bear witness of His saving power. The "what ifs" grab us by the throat and snag our tongue. *What if I can't pay my bills or buy what I want?* are nagging thoughts as we step out to obey Christ financially. *What if I lose a friend, a date, or acceptance in the group? What if righteousness takes all the fun out of life? What if I have to suffer in obedience? What if God does not provide?* The unknown looms as a large obstacle that threatens to block basic simple obedience, leave us spiritual zeroes, and make us little more than stagnant ponds.

FOUR OBSTACLES

So far we have seen that for every good plan of God to bless us, Satan responds with some kind of counterattack. It's no different with God's three-dimensional process. The account of Abraham and Sarah in Hebrews 11 delineates four obstacles that threaten to block the progress of God's process.

Fear of the Unknown

When threatened by the fear of the unknown, we must remember all that God is and all He promises to be. The one sure known in the unknown is that God is there. Hebrews 11:8 tells us that Abraham hurdled this first obstacle by faith. He was willing to believe in God and trust Him no matter what.

When my children were smaller, Martie and I would often surprise them with special family nights out. I'd walk in the door and say, "Tonight we are going out for a surprise." Do you think they began to cry, hide in corners of the room, or plead with me not to take them into the unknown? Not on your life! They would run and jump for joy, grab their coats, and want to leave as soon as possible. How could they so cheerfully face the unknown? They trusted their father!

The psalmist says, "Taste and see that the Lord is good; blessed is the man who takes refuge in him. Fear the Lord, you his saints, for those who fear him lack nothing" (Psalm 34:8–9). To His disciples, Christ said, "Do not worry, saying, 'What shall we eat?' or 'What shall we drink?' or 'What shall we wear?' For the pagans run after all these things, and your heavenly Father knows that you need them. But seek first his kingdom and his righteousness, and all these things will be given to you as well" (Matthew 6:31–33).

As we experience the goodness of God and place our trust in Him, we learn to deal with the fear of the unknown. Yet like the hurdler who leaps successfully over one hurdle and immediately faces another, we will find that Satan places additional hurdles in front of us as we step out with God.

Past Comforts

The second obstacle we can expect is the pull of past comforts. Abraham and his family were called to be nomads as they followed God to where He wanted them to go (Hebrews 11:9, 13). If they had given too much thought to their past and the land from which they came, they may have gone back (Hebrews 11:15).

I can almost see it now, Abraham pacing in front of the tent and Sarah asking him what's wrong. He replies, "Don't you know what time it is? The guys are teeing off right now at the Chaldee Country Club. I miss it so much, Sarah . . . Let's go back!" To which Sarah replies, "I know how you feel, Abe. Cooking over this charcoal fire makes me miss my microwave—and besides, my tennis game will never be the same again. Turn the camels around. My bags are already packed!"

When the process of spiritual growth demands leaving a sinful habit behind, there will be the pull of its memory, of its temporary satisfaction. Obedience to God may demand lowering our comfort level to live a simpler, less materialistic existence, and the pull of past standards of living will threaten to bring the process to a quick halt. Missionaries experience this pull. So do Christian workers who must subsist on meager salaries. Persons called from lucrative businesses into kingdom work may struggle with it as well.

Why did Abraham and Sarah persist in the process? Because "they were longing for a better country—a heavenly one" (Hebrews 11:16). Their values were beyond the shallow "here and now." They had their hearts in the right place—in eternal realities. They were citizens of a better land.

The story is told of an elderly couple who had given their lives sacrificially as God's missionaries in foreign service. Their health declined to the point that their mission board called them home to retirement. On their ship were an ambassador and his wife who were returning home to retire as well. As the ship slipped through the Atlantic, the missionary couple watched the ambassador as he drank and partied. They heard his boisterous laughter and noticed his often crude behavior.

As the boat pulled into port, the missionaries noticed a crowd of people on the dock. The gangplank went down and an important-looking man came onto the boat to escort the ambassador and his wife to the dock. A crowd gathered around the public figure. Cameras flashed. The ambassador received a medal and his wife was presented with a dozen roses. Meanwhile, God's representatives picked their way through the crowd. They too were home, but no one was there to meet them. As they walked silently toward the baggage claim area, tears were running down the missionary wife's cheeks. Her husband tenderly asked, "What's wrong?" She replied, "All of these years of serving the Lord, and now we come home and there's no one here. No medals for you, no roses for me." He thought for a moment and then pulled her close and said, "Honey, we're not home yet!"

This was a man in process who escaped the destructive gravity of "creature comforts" and rewards. We too need to persistently march toward home . . . that better place.

Believing the Impossible

If we can overcome the pull of past comforts, some of us will come face-to-face with the third hurdle, the impossible. Abraham and Sarah obeyed by faith and persisted by valuing eternal realities, but then their productivity was threatened by being asked to believe the impossible. With Sarah past childbearing age, it was impossible for them to produce a family as God had promised. When God finally told Abraham the time had come for him to have a son, he laughed (Genesis 17:17). Sarah laughed as well (Genesis 18:12). Impossible! "Who, me?"

If you were asked to appear before the President of the United States, there would be a certain protocol you would be expected to follow. It wouldn't be wise to bounce unannounced into his office and shout, "Hey, Prez, what's up!" There is protocol with God, as well. There are some words you should never use in His presence, and *impossible* is one of them. It's not in His vocabulary.

Obedience to God often moves us into the territory of the impossible. Think of Israel with the Red Sea in front of them and the Egyptian army racing up from behind . . . Shadrach and friends taking a casual stroll in the fiery furnace . . . Daniel waiting for morning in the lion's den . . . Christ conquering death in the tomb . . . Peter walking, unchained and unstopped, from between guards in the heart of a dark prison. When God does the impossible, then and only then can He show the extent of His strength on our behalf. That's how He demonstrates His glory to a watching world. He delights in the impossible.

I am convinced that God wanted to reveal to Abraham and Sarah what kind of God He was, so He let them slip out of the possible and into the impossible. Isaac was more than *their* child. He became a living reminder that God faithfully keeps His promises even when it seems impossible to do so. Isaac was a symbol of God's strength, of His continuing purpose in their lives. Nothing is impossible with God (Genesis 18:14; Philippians 4:13).

Lack of Immediate Gratification

Lastly, the process of spiritual growth is difficult because there is seldom instant feedback. Abraham and Sarah died without having received many of the promises of God (Hebrews 11:13). Several of the promises made in Genesis 12:1–3 would be fulfilled beyond the scope of their own lifetimes. The promises of a great nation, a great name, a land to call his own, and a Messiah all hinged on Abraham's faithfulness to the process—yet he saw none of these come to pass before he died. Abraham's faith and obedience were investments for *future* dividends. Abraham was a person determined to stay in the process for the bigger picture.

Susanna Wesley, mother of John and Charles Wesley, was a woman of the bigger picture. She had nineteen children and a husband who was of little or no help. She stuck it out and taught each child God's Word. Do you think she was ever tempted to pack her bags and tell God, "I wanted a family, not an orphanage! I quit!"? Little did she know that two of her boys would become dynamic spiritual leaders for the kingdom of Christ in the British Isles.

A graduate of a small midwestern Bible college felt led to try to start a church in a northern logging camp. He stepped out with God and became a man in process. He heard the people taunt him: "A Sunday school *here?* This is a tough place, preacher. We don't need a Sunday school." Door after door was slammed in his face.

But he persisted. Finally, behind one of those doors was a young boy who asked permission to go to Sunday school. Then another boy went as well.

Those two boys accepted Christ and went on to attend Bible college. Afterward, one went into missions and the other into youth work. The missionary went to Bangladesh to pioneer a work where a doctor recently converted from agnosticism to Christianity would establish a hospital. This doctor in turn would write his life story in a book that would stimulate hundreds of people to go into missions work for God. As a result of reading *Daktar,* many others would accept Christ.

The youth worker was also blessed by God. He ascended to national recognition and impacted thousands of young people for Christ. Only eternity will tell the full story of what God was able to do with one life in a logging camp. Even with no instant feedback, this life was persistent in the process and productive far beyond itself.

Abraham and Sarah were *bigger-picture people*. They were willing to be down payments, investments, seeds planted for productivity in God's larger plan. Therefore, the lack of instant feedback did not deter them. They obeyed, persisted, and produced—in God's time.

When we step out with God, we must do so in faith, believing that He is the known in the unknown. We must develop an unflinching belief that He is the God of the impossible. Our commitment is not to the here and now, but to the bigger picture. These things fortify our persistence and guarantee productivity.

GOD'S KIND OF PEOPLE

All my life I've been urged not to be ashamed of God, but on occasion I have wondered whether He might be ashamed of me. I can think of no greater privilege than to know that He'd be pleased to claim me as His own. I'd like to think that He would stop all of heaven, call the angels around His throne, part the clouds, and point to me, saying, "That's My kind of man!"

Stepping out with God in obedience, persistence, and productivity won that accolade from God for Abraham and Sarah. The book of Hebrews says, "God is not ashamed to be called their God" (Hebrews 11:16).

Though Sarah and Abraham had momentary failures and shortcomings (as we shall soon see), over the long haul they played a key role in the kingdom conflict. By God's grace and occasional sovereign intervention, they fulfilled their part in their time to provide the Savior for us. They became mobile for God. He led them where He wanted them to be, they obeyed, and we are blessed today. It is now our turn to step out with God as they did, to play *our* part in the promotion of the Messiah message, and to be victorious for Him in the conflict.

Stepping out with God is always stepping up!

Questions for Your Personal Conflict

1. Because Abraham and Sarah obeyed God and decided to move, their lives took on wonderful new potential. What was the last move or decision you made that changed your life dramatically?

2. Are you currently considering a move or decision that could have a major effect on your life? If so, who are three people (whose opinions matter to you) whom you could consult for trustworthy advice?

3. Which of the obstacles to spiritual growth seems to affect you most strongly? Why?
   ___ Fear of the unknown   ___ Past comforts
   ___ Believing the impossible   ___ Lack of immediate gratification

4. What would you say are the symptoms of spiritual stagnation? When you see these symptoms in your own life, what do you do to get back in a growth cycle again?

5. Create a simple spiritual growth chart for your life. Place age increments horizontally across the bottom, and let the vertical axis indicate spiritual maturity (the higher, the more mature; the lower, the more stagnation). Use this graph to review your past times of spiritual growth, decline, and stagnation. However, keep in mind that this is all behind you now. Spend time in prayer seeking God's help in making the *future* a time of continual spiritual growth.

8

FOR LACK OF CONVICTION, THE BATTLE WAS LOST

The Battle Against Fear

I t used to be when you saw those blue signs with the wheelchairs on them, the ones in the parking lot closest to the door, the word that came to mind was *handicapped*. The designated parking spaces, the addition of ramps for wheelchair accessibility, and the redesign of buildings, water fountains, telephones, and such have been signs of our growing awareness that many in our society are disabled. The cripplers are varied—war, accidents, heart disease, cancer, birth defects, and on goes the list. Being disabled means living with certain limitations, such as lost dreams, a fear of never being whole again, or a constant comparison to a world of people whose potential is unhindered. Yet since nothing can be done to remedy the situation in most cases, we have been urged to think of such people not as *handicapped*, but rather as *physically challenged*.

Within the kingdom of Christ, the disabled number more than a few. The "spiritually challenged" live with limitations and untapped potential. They have come to believe that they are unable to witness, to give, to go to the mission field, to cease their worry and anxiety, to forgive, to spend time with their families, to love their enemies, to pray and study the Word, to encourage and help the hurting, to be positive. These are people who are truly handicapped. It's not that they are *unable* to do these things; they are usually just *unwilling*. They handicap themselves. In the midst of the kingdom conflict, it seems that many soldiers of Christ are "Can't do" Christians . . . crippled . . . easy prey for the adversary.

THE CRIPPLER—FEAR

Though the cripplers are many, few of Satan's weapons are more powerful or more prevalent than fear.

On our way home from a vacation in Florida, we stopped at a multistoried motel just south of Atlanta. With the family settled in, I went down to the lobby to buy some snacks. Suddenly, fire alarms were blaring. Word spread quickly that fire had broken out on one of the upper floors. I climbed the nearest stairway to help my family evacuate. As I ran up the stairwell, the smoke became dense. I burst onto our floor and found the room empty. They had already gone! Relieved and hoping that they had made it out, I ran down to the parking lot. There they were, Martie and the children. Martie had grabbed our youngest child in her arms and the two others by the hand. But as she began her descent, her legs had become weak and shaky—so much so that she could no longer go down the stairs and carry the baby at the same time. She feared she would not make it out. But just then a man came by, offered to carry the baby, and went ahead. Martie took off her shoes for better stability and made it out safely.

Fear is a powerful emotion. Witnesses of major tragedies often testify that people are immobilized by fear. When caught before a subway train, victims will often freeze on the spot instead of running to safety. Some who live to tell about their brush with death say, "I couldn't move!" That's what it means to be scared stiff.

Franklin D. Roosevelt was right when he proclaimed, "The only thing we have to fear is fear itself." On a spiritual level, fear intimidates, immobilizes, and renders us dysfunctional.

FEAR IN PERSPECTIVE

Fear is not always bad. In the right context, it can be a true ally. If you were in the woods with any angry bear hot on your trail, fear would be a great stimulus to run for cover. A healthy fear of spiritual failure, the consequence of sin, the reality of our adversary, and the judgment of God should motivate us to pursue the safety and security of all that is right and good. But when fear begins to separate us from God and His plan, we must become concerned.

Christ spoke often to His disciples about the crippling nature of fear. He was concerned that their fear of inadequate provisions (such as food and clothes) would distract them from being attentive to the primary importance of the kingdom in their lives (Luke 12:22–32). He was also concerned that the fear of danger would disable them from courageously proclaiming the message of the Messiah (Matthew 10:26–31). The first fear threatened to interrupt their church-planting careers and send them back to their nets. The second could potentially silence their witness. Fear threatened to make the disciples displaced persons with displaced potential.

Moving through the book of Genesis, we don't get far before we see the weapon of fear marshaled against the promised kingdom of Christ. As early as Genesis 12 and again in Genesis 20, Satan used fear in an attempt to neutralize the effectiveness of Abraham and Sarah. His plan was effective to a large degree when Abraham, in need of basic supply and protection in the face of danger, responded with fear instead of trust and courage.

The kingdom conflict becomes more focused in Genesis 12. Prior to that point, all of mankind had been a possible threat to Satan's survival. The "seed of woman" was universal in scope. In Genesis 12, however, God narrowed the promise to a particular person and his family line. That person was Abraham.

Abraham was promised that he would have a land (Genesis 12:1, 7); that through him a great nation would be born (v. 2); and that through him the Messiah would come, "and all peoples on earth will be blessed" (Genesis 12:3; Gal. 3:8, 16). In the light of this divine announcement, Satan's efforts will be focused on Abraham and Sarah. They are God's, and Satan will do whatever he can to quench the potential through them.

Two things are important at this moment in the history of the conflict—the place and the people. God planned for the Messiah to be born in a particular place, so Abraham had to leave his home to establish himself in God's place (Genesis 12:1, 7). While they were in this place, God would focus on them as people. God would give them a child through which a great nation would come (12:2; 15:4;

18:10). If Satan's dominion was to prevail, he must displace them from the land and displace the seed of Sarah (3:15; 15:4; 18:10). Fear would be his weapon.

DISPLACED PERSONS

On two different occasions Abraham faced famine in the land where God had placed him. Both times he packed his bags, apparently without much thought. He traveled once to Egypt (Genesis 12) and a second time to the greener pastures of King Abimelech's country (Genesis 20). The land is central to God's plan. Yet, with almost no struggle, Satan displaced Abraham and Sarah from God's place for them because Abraham feared for basic supply.

We cannot fault Abraham for being concerned. Food is of ultimate importance. Yet Abraham was God's man in God's place. Did he really think God would let him starve to death? Possibly Abraham did not yet have enough faith to trust God for supply. But as Abraham drove past the "Leaving Canaan" sign, he eliminated the opportunity for God to prove Himself trustworthy.

Just think of God's options. He could have made the parched ground blossom around Abraham's feet. He could have sent ravens with food as He did for Elijah. He could have provided some early form of manna. Whatever the method, God had made promises to Abraham, and He certainly was not going to let His man starve to death in the meantime. Had Abraham stayed, it would have strengthened his faith through a firsthand experience with God's might. And it would have provided a powerful witness to the pagan Canaanites that Abraham's God was the true and living God.

But that's not the way the story goes. Abraham took matters into his own hands and went looking for food. In doing so, he forfeited both personal growth and testimony to the living God.

His story has been repeated a thousand times through a thousand other lives. Even today many people separate themselves from the will of God because they fear for the basics of life and try to deal with the problem themselves rather than trusting God. And since we live in such an affluent society, our fear has escalated beyond the fear of not having *what we need* into a fear of not having *all we want*. Contentment is a disappearing quality in the Christian community.

Think of the person who begins to consider that God's place may be some type of ministry or service. What about his dreams of a home in a nice neighborhood, a sporty car, and a comfortable salary? How could he ask his wife and family to do without all the things that "everybody else" has? The fear of supply derails him; he becomes a displaced person.

Consider the businessman who has the opportunity to climb the corporate ladder. More money. Better supply. But the promotion means moving to a new city, spending more time away from his family, and leaving the church where he has a teaching ministry and where there is a strong bond of fellowship and support. Will he even consider staying where he is, trusting in God's continued supply? Or does he automatically make the move, sacrificing the values of the kingdom for the fear of less supply?

What about the pastor whose congregation forces humility on him by keeping his salary low? Can he be content with what he has, trusting in God's supply (Philippians 4:19; 1 Timothy 6:6–12)? Or will he pack his bags and move on to greener pastures?

Think of the Christians whose top priority in life is to make enough money to have all they need and want. As a result, they have nothing left for the kingdom of Christ. Fearing loss of their buying potential, they disobey God's commands to first give of their resources to the kingdom work of Christ (Proverbs 3:9). These too are displaced persons—displaced by fear from the sphere of obedience and blessing, from fellowship with God.

SIMPLY TRUSTING

What Abraham lacked was trust . . . confidence in God as a God of supply. Trust is consistently cited in Scripture as the antidote to fear:

- "When I am afraid, I will trust in you" (Psalm 56:3).
- "The lions may grow weak and hungry, but those who seek the Lord lack no good thing" (Psalm 34:10).
- "The Lord redeems his servants; no one will be condemned who takes refuge in him" (Psalm 34:22).
- "I was young and now I am old, yet I have never seen the

righteous forsaken or their children begging bread" (Psalm 37:25).

• "My God will meet all your needs according to his glorious riches in Christ Jesus" (Philippians 4:19).

People who claim these scriptural realities rebuke the fear of supply and are free to seek first the kingdom of God. We become followers of Christ, who taught:

> Do not worry about your life, what you will eat; or about your body, what you will wear. Life is more than food, and the body more than clothes. Consider the ravens: They do not sow or reap, they have no storeroom or barn; yet God feeds them. And how much more valuable you are than birds! Who of you by worrying can add a single hour to his life? Since you cannot do this very little thing, why do you worry about the rest? Consider how the lilies grow. They do not labor or spin. Yet I tell you, not even Solomon in all his splendor was dressed like one of these. If that is how God clothes the grass of the field, which is here today, and tomorrow is thrown into the fire, how much more will he clothe you, O you of little faith! And do not set your heart on what you will eat or drink; do not worry about it. For the pagan world runs after all such things, and your Father knows that you need them. But seek his kingdom, and these things will be given to you as well. Do not be afraid, little flock, for your Father has been pleased to give you the kingdom. (Luke 12:22–32)

Disciples who trust God refuse to be displaced. As a result we experience firsthand God's miraculous power supply and provide proof to a watching world that God is real (Psalm 67). In fact, when faced with want and when our supply is threatened, we are on miracle territory as long as we remain where God has placed us. My own family has experienced this time and time again. With God we have nothing to fear. And in the place of fear comes a thrilling anticipation of God's supply—in His way, in His time. God always has options we've never dreamed of!

When we encounter times of want and short supply, God may be doing any number of things in our lives, including:

• tearing away our self-sufficiency to prove again that He is our only true resource.

- redefining our values. As long as we trust in Him, the significance of family, friends, spiritual realities, His Word, and prayer come back into focus.
- teaching us to be resourceful and diligent with what we have.
- giving us the opportunity to reevaluate our earning and spending habits so that slothfulness and overspending may be eliminated.
- reminding us of the difference between needs and wants.

COMFORTABLY DISPLACED

Prosperity is not always a sign of God's blessing. Even after Abraham moved to Egypt rather than trusting God, he prospered. Satan, at this point, saw to it that Abraham was not only displaced, but locked into his displacement with ease and affluence. We are told that Pharaoh "treated Abram well for [Sarai's] sake, and Abram acquired sheep and cattle, male and female donkeys, menservants and maidservants, and camels" (Genesis 12:16).

If God had not intervened, Abraham might have settled down and enjoyed the favor of Pharaoh in a location other than God's place for him. When displaced persons become wealthy and comfortable, it becomes even more difficult for them to return to God's plan.

If we are displaced and comfortable, getting back to where God wants us to be may mean relinquishing some of our comforts. But that would be no sacrifice. If it comes down to one or the other, it is far better to be at ease with God than to be comfortable in the world.

I like Moses' perspective. Moses "chose to be mistreated along with the people of God rather than to enjoy the pleasures of sin for a short time. He regarded disgrace for the sake of Christ as of greater value than the treasures of Egypt, because he was looking ahead to his reward" (Hebrews 11:25–27).

I can't help but wonder how many believers are spiritually handicapped because they are comfortably displaced. Self-sufficiency is almost always associated with affluence and apathy. It displaces people from God's place for them, and they no longer are willing to give to their church, go to the mission field, witness for Christ regularly, or exercise their gifts in the body of Christ. They miss so much because they fear they might become less comfortable, less affluent, less at ease. I am reminded of Paul's sad commentary on one of his associates who had become displaced: "Demas, because he loved this world, has deserted me" (2 Timothy 4:10).

DISPLACED POTENTIAL

Not only was it Satan's goal to displace Abraham and Sarah from the land, but he also wanted to displace the potential of the seed they had been promised (Genesis 3:15; 12:2–3). If it weren't for the promised seed, Abraham and Sarah's location would have been insignificant. In Genesis 12 we can only assume that Sarah is to be the seed bearer, but all doubt is removed by the time we get to the account in Genesis 20. By then God had made it clear that Sarah would be the one through whom the promised victor would come (Genesis 18:10).

Because he faithlessly displaced himself from where God had led him, Abraham created a dilemma for himself. Evidently Sarah was a striking woman (Genesis 12:11–12). She was desired first by Pharaoh (12:14–16) and then by Abimelech (20:2). Both of these were very powerful men, and they were also very moral—in a sense. They would never steal another man's wife, because that would be wrong. But they would have no qualms about killing the man and then treating his widow with kindness. This was an accepted cultural practice of the time.

It is not without reason that Abraham was afraid. Knowing that he might be killed simply because his wife was beautiful, Abraham made a pact with Sarah to say that she was his sister (they *were* half-brother and sister). If the leaders of the nation had no interest in Sarah, there would be no harm. But if they did, Abraham's life would be spared—even if it meant Sarah would be added to the king's harem.

Fearful people are often selfish people. Abraham selfishly "solved" his dilemma by risking the reputation of his own wife and potentially forfeiting the relationship they had developed over the years. Even if we want to give him the benefit of the doubt that he expected nothing to happen, we learn differently. Pharaoh certainly did everything in his power to "court" Sarah (Genesis 12:10–20). If God hadn't intervened, Abraham would have lost his wife then. Yet he was willing to use the same self-protecting strategy later, in the land of King Abimelech. He intentionally chose to dwell safely, even if singly, in a foreign land.

What is significant here is that fear has placed the Messiah seed in a foreign king's harem. Satan first used the fear of inadequate supply to displace Abraham and Sarah from the land, and then the fear of danger to displace the potential seed.

Things appear bleak for God's kingdom. Twice now, in its early stages, God's people are not in God's place and appear willing to forfeit the potential of the Messiah promise through them. This has been a masterful bit of strategy for Satan. With fear as a centerpiece, Satan targets a man who trustlessly asserts his self-sufficiency and spinelessly puts self-preservation before his wife and, more significantly, before the great cause of God (12:13).

Like Abraham, we too are vulnerable to sacrificing the potential of God through us by responding to a dangerous world with self-protecting cowardice. Fearing the loss of a sale, a businessperson sacrifices her biblical convictions so she is not rejected by a client. A pastor, fearing the loss of congregational respect, softens the truth and stills the prophetic urging of his heart and conscience. A new Christian ignores opportunities to witness in order to save face with lost friends and family members. Fearing rejection by their children, parents renege on teaching biblical standards of righteousness. Whenever we allow fear to control us, the potential of God through us is displaced.

What does God expect? Martyrs? Perhaps! But above all, God expects unconditional commitment. My mind races when I think of the thrilling story of Shadrach, Meshach, and Abednego, who refused to flinch, even in the face of great danger. Consider their words before the world ruler who was in a fit of rage because they would not bow down to his image:

> O Nebuchadnezzar, we do not need to defend ourselves before you in this matter. If we are thrown into the blazing furnace, the God we serve is able to save us from it, and he will rescue us from your hand, O king. But even if he does not, we want you to know, O king, that

we will not serve your gods or worship the image of gold you have set up. (Daniel 3:16–18)

Shadrach, Meshach, and Abednego, because of their courageous obedience to God, were thrown into the fiery furnace. But they discovered that was God's place for them. God miraculously delivered them. Their potential was unlocked in the fire. As a result, the reality of the true and living God was displayed for Nebuchadnezzar to see firsthand. This proud, pagan king acknowledged God as the "Most High God" (Daniel 3:26–30). This could never have happened if Shadrach, Meshach, and Abednego had chosen the option of self-sufficiency and self-protection rather than an uncompromising obedience to God.

Stephen had a similar commitment, but a different result. His unflinching commitment to God led to his death. But even in death he radiated a testimony for his persecutors to see and hear (Acts 7:54–8:3). The young man holding the garments for those who stoned Stephen soon had a dramatic conversion and became Paul the apostle. I often wonder if at that moment God didn't begin a work of pre-evangelism in Paul's life that would prepare him for the Damascus road experience (Acts 9:1–31). For the believer, dying is gain and an entrance into all that is far better (Philippians 1:21, 23)—and often the unlocking of God's potential.

Healing the Handicapped

A friend of mine jokes that great miracles are taking place in parking lots all over America. He says that he often sees a car pull into a place marked for handicapped people and the people emerge from the car absolutely whole, fully healed.

We need some healing in the body of Christ from this crippler of fear. An unconditional commitment to the principles of Christ's kingdom demands courage—courage to trust God for His supply in the face of our needs, and for His sovereign supervision in the face of danger.

The Almighty God is always with us. We will never face a situation where He leaves us to fend on our own. The presence of God is the key to our courage. Look at God's exhortation to Joshua:

Be strong and courageous, because you will lead these people to inherit the land I swore to their forefathers to give them. Be strong and very courageous. Be careful to obey all the law my servant Moses gave you; do not turn from it to the right or to the left, that you may be successful wherever you go. Do not let this Book of the Law depart from your mouth; meditate on it day and night, so that you may be careful to do everything written in it. Then you will be prosperous and successful. Have I not commanded you? Be strong and courageous. Do not be terrified; do not be discouraged, for the Lord your God will be with you wherever you go. (Joshua 1:6–9)

God is with you—and that makes all the difference in the world. If He is with you, what is there to fear? Even Satan's power does not match His (1 John 4:4). The writer to the Hebrews says it so well, "'Never will [God] leave you; never will [He] forsake you.' So we say with confidence, 'The Lord is my helper; I will not be afraid. What can man do to me?'" (Hebrews 13:5–6). There is no reason to become displaced because of fear. If God stands for us and with us to supply and protect, who can be against us (Romans 8:31–39)?

As a boy I learned that being in the right company dispels fear. I remember visiting a church on a Sunday evening in one of the worst sections of New York City. Our family parked a block or so away. As we walked, fear grew steadily in my heart. Thankfully, we made it safely to the church and enjoyed the service. After the service, the pastor asked two of his deacons to escort us back to the car. They looked like the church "bouncers." Though it was dark outside, I had no fear. What made the difference? The presence of those who could protect me.

Fear also abates when we experience the companionship of Christian friends who encourage us to be courageous. A little girl was crying in her bed after her dad had prayed with her and turned out the lights. Her concerned father told her not to be afraid. "Jesus is with you," he said. She continued to sob, "But, Daddy, I'm still afraid." He reminded her, "Honey, you need to know that Jesus is right here in this room with you. You shouldn't be afraid." Finally she said through her sobs, "I know, Daddy, but I want somptin' that's got skin on it."

God knows we need each other! That's what the church is all

about. Are you fearful? Find fellowship with those who are coura-geously righteous, who trust unflinchingly in the supply and protec-tion of God. Spend time with them. Let them model courage for you. And then in your strength, be "somptin' that's got skin on it" for someone else.

THE KINGDOM RESTORED

God's plan, left to Abraham and Sarah, lost its place and potential. Yet God remains sovereign. He stepped in with His theo-cratic intervention to restore their ability to be in His place and ful-fill His potential through them. God used a series of plagues against Pharaoh to alert him to the fact of Sarah's true identity as Abraham's wife (Genesis 12:17). King Abimelech experienced a serious illness (20:3, 17) and the shutdown of the entire reproduc-tive capabilities of his household (v. 17). No one was able to con-ceive while Sarah was in that house, and as long as the king was dreadfully ill he would have no sexual interest in her (v. 4). Sarah, who trusted God (1 Peter 3:4–6), was divinely protected both times and restored to her husband.

Though fear had won the battle, God again won the war. The seed of woman, the promised Messiah, twice threatened by fear, was twice restored by the hand of a faithful and sovereign God.

Questions for Your Personal Conflict

1. What were your childhood fears? How did you eventually overcome them?

2. What, if any, are your fears as an adult? To what extent do your fears control your actions? Have you ever been completely incapacitated by fear?

3. Abraham's fear seemed to have more of an effect on Sarah than on himself. In what ways, if any, do your fears have the potential to affect others you care about?

4. What are three Bible references—from this chapter or elsewhere—that you would find comforting in a fearful situation? After you identify them, why not commit them to memory so they will come to mind the next time fear threatens to exert too much control over you?

5. What do you think you might accomplish for God if you had absolutely no fear? What steps can you take to reduce your level of fear in order to increase your level of commitment to Him?

9

ACTING WITHOUT ORDERS
The Battle Against Impatience

I love the prayer "Lord, make me more patient—and do it right now!" Many people cite patience as one of their most difficult spiritual assignments. Striving to develop patience is complicated by the fact that almost everything around us is instant—money from ATM machines, microwaved food, overnight delivery, etc. Credit, communication, media, entertainment, and hundreds of other items are available almost immediately simply by dialing an 800 number.

So only when we are *forced* to wait for something do we learn how well we are doing with the elusive virtue of patience. Grade yourself: How well do you handle waiting when the car in front of you doesn't respond to a light turned green? To a slow cashier at the grocery store? To an extra long wait at the doctor's office?

Other times the stakes are far higher. How do you respond while anxiously waiting for a needed check, a longed-for phone call, or a doctor's report after serious surgery? Have you ever waited for a job when unemployed, or with a loved one suffering with a terminal illness? It's a struggle to be locked in the waiting room of life—a room that appears to have no windows or doors . . . a trap with seemingly no escape . . . a tunnel with no end. It's a vulnerable place to be.

But in addition to being hard and frustrating, waiting makes us vulnerable to Satan's attack. We are drawn toward choices that lead us into Satan's grasp. Many times those hastily made choices do irreparable damage.

THE IMPATIENCE PROCESS

Such was the case with Abraham and Sarah in Genesis 16. Unwilling to wait for God to complete His will, in His way, in His time, they jumped in and took over. If we take a close look at their situation and their responses, we will discover several reasons for failure that are all rooted in impatience. We are just as susceptible to these things today as they were long ago. There are four basic factors that make us vulnerable to impatience and consequent failure.

The Delayed Promises Factor

Much impatience relates directly to our expectations. When we expect something to happen and it doesn't occur, we feel the tension of an impatient spirit. This is especially true if the expectation is important to us.

Many of our expectations are a result of promises we have received from other people, or even from God. Abraham had been promised a son (Genesis 15:4–6). This was an important promise because in his day childlessness was cause for shame and humiliation. Abraham and Sarah's pride was at stake. What would people think?

In the perspective of the kingdom conflict, this promised son was significant because he would be the next step in the fulfillment of the Messiah promise (3:15; 12:3). As far as Satan knew, Abraham's child may even have been the Messiah. So Satan attempted to capitalize on Sarah's impatience by placing a substitute son in Abraham's house. After years passed with no sign of the son God had promised, Sarah's impatience made her vulnerable to other alternatives when she should have stood firm on the promises of God.

God has provided us with a Book full of promises. He promises us provision, protection, and His presence and perseverance. God expects us to wait for the fulfillment of these promises. How well we wait is one measure of our spiritual maturity.

The Possibilities Factor

Right on the heels of the promise factor is the possibility factor. When God's promises don't come to pass as we think they should, we tend to lose patience with Him. We start considering all the possibilities *we* can think of to work our own way out of the situation we face.

After Sarah waited for several years without yet having a child of her own, she felt that God had restrained her from bearing children (Genesis 16:2). She assumed, however, that God would *always* prevent her from this privilege, which was a misassumption. What she had forgotten, or perhaps never realized, is that all things are possible with God (18:14). In fact, God delights in putting us in impossible situations so that He might prove Himself strong (2 Chronicles 16:9).

Sarah assumed that God had put her in a room without doors. She had waited long enough. She felt she had to make her own plans, cut her own way out. That was exactly what Satan wanted her to think.

The Plan-B Factor

When promises remain unfulfilled and we continue to peruse all the possibilities that make sense to us, many times we become firm believers in the old adage "The Lord helps those who help themselves." At this point in the process, Sarah decided to "help" the Lord by giving Abraham her maidservant, Hagar. Culturally, this was a common practice. As a result, Hagar bore a son, Ishmael. Abraham loved him and wanted him to be the son God had promised (Genesis 17:18). But he wasn't.

In their impatience, Abraham and Sarah had determined their own way to keep God's promise. They did it their way in their time. As a result, Satan had diverted God's line of victory. The seed of Christ's kingdom now had a counterfeit. Satan used a well-meant plan which had been generated in impatience, and he capitalized on it with little or no struggle.

In our cultural atmosphere of independence and self-assertiveness, we too fall easy prey to this "Plan-B" factor. We even do good things in our way and in our time. But by preempting God's plan and God's timing, we miss out on the *best* that can happen to us.

The Problem Factor

From the moment Hagar became pregnant, problems set in. Sarah became so uncontrollably jealous that Hagar had to run for her life (Genesis 16:6). Abraham was torn between a feuding Hagar and Sarah. After weighing all the possibilities, their plan had seemed to make so much sense. But now they had to deal with a bigger problem than ever.

What seemed so right to Abraham and Sarah gave Satan a handle, a sword against the kingdom of Christ. The results of their impatient act have continued through the generations of history right up to our own. The descendants of Ishmael became the Arab peoples. The Israelites were the descendants of Isaac, as are the modern-day Jews. The ongoing tension between these two groups of people affects world peace and strains the best of diplomacy. Satan has used the religion of the Arab world, Islam, to wage actual war against Christians. Today, followers of Islam are one of the hardest, most militant groups when it comes to opposing the Gospel of Christ.

A young associate minister owned an old used car, and it was hard on his ego to park it in the church lot Sunday after Sunday. After some deliberation, he stretched himself financially and bought a new car. As he slid from behind the wheel in the parking lot the next Sunday, a man approached him and said, "I see you have a new car. My wife and I had just decided this week that we wanted to give you a car. But I'm sure we can find someone else who needs one."

This young pastor regretfully realized that his purchase had unwisely placed him under much financial pressure. The newness of the car would soon be gone and he would face the reality that there was too much month at the end of the money. Financial pressure always distracts us from God's best. It puts tension into marriages, gives us a "money focus" in our lives, and keeps us from being generous for Christ's kingdom work.

Not only are we impatient financially, but emotionally as well. Our nation's high divorce rate is a tragic reminder of our impatience. Certainly many marriages could be saved if both spouses exercised patience on a regular basis.

A woman who had been divorced only a few months asked my advice about marrying again. I felt she hadn't given the situation enough time, and I asked her to reconsider. But in a few weeks she remarried anyway. That very same weekend I received word that her ex-husband had come back to the Lord and was seeking forgiveness from both God and his wife. He wanted to restore his marriage. I had to bear the bad news—it was too late. Think of the loss: of influence on coming generations, of great victory and testimony to the power of Christ to heal, and to the heart of a man who got right with God and found himself locked out of what he treasured most in life.

That woman had God's promise of His chastening work in her husband's life (Proverbs 3:11–12) and of His provision for her needs. Sometimes God expects us to wait for Him to work (Psalm 27:14). In this case His work had already begun, unseen, in the heart of the woman's ex-mate. Yet the situation seemed impossible to her, so she went ahead with her own plan because it seemed so right, so easy, so comfortable.

Running ahead of God always has consequences. When we become impatient with God, we become vulnerable to Satan's attack. This vulnerability extends even to our day-to-day decisions.

God may use our lack of ready cash to keep us from buying some item that will distract us from Him and from spiritual growth. Can we be patient or will we please ourselves and purchase it with instant credit? A wife may become impatient with God's work in her husband's life and begin to manipulate and pressure him, which only serves to alienate his spirit from both her and God. A Christian may zealously commit to the disciplines of Bible study and prayer, expecting instant results and spiritual power. When spiritual growth doesn't come quickly, the tendency is to reject the disciplines because they don't work fast enough. Consequently, the person is left without the vital resources of spiritual food and fellowship with God.

How do we learn to wait patiently before God? Two basic principles provide the peace necessary to wait confidently for Him and guard ourselves against the negative impact of impatience.

GOD WAITS WITH PURPOSE

Once when my son Matthew was younger, I called for him to help me with something important. I expected his presence immediately, but he didn't come. I called again. He called back, "Just a minute, Dad." I called a third time, with more intensity. He yelled, "I'll be right there." As the moments passed, I felt the emotional and physical effects of my rightful impatience. As I stewed, he finally came running. Out of breath and with a tender fear in his eyes, he explained why he hadn't come immediately. Upon explanation, I realized that what he was doing was just as important as what I needed him for. When I understood his reason for delaying, I relaxed and my peace of mind returned.

Relating to God is very much like that. If we understand *why* God doesn't come rushing to our side every time we call Him, we can learn to wait patiently for Him. There are at least three reasons why God waits before responding to us.

1. God waits for the sake of our growth.

I don't know about you, but much of my spiritual growth takes place during crisis situations. When everything is going well, I am tempted to coast. Prosperity without pain doesn't do much to motivate my spiritual life. But let some crisis hit and immediately I become sensitive to God. I reflect carefully about the condition of my life and find myself praying for insight and guidance. When God oversees our spiritual growth, the process often includes pressure and always takes time (Romans 5:3–5; James 1:2–4). If we are to learn to wait patiently through trouble, we must learn to focus on our growth and the joy of increasing Christlikeness. We discover the pain we experience has purpose and the growth is worth the wait.

David was frequently in God's "waiting room," but probably never more than when he was on the run from King Saul. Psalm 13 echoes the agony he felt from being placed in the waiting room, a cave, while Saul's army searched for him to take his life. David cried to God, "How long, O Lord? Will you forget me forever? How long will you hide your face from me? How long must I wrestle with my thoughts and every day have sorrow in my heart? How long will my enemy triumph over me?" (Psalm 13:1–2).

David had been faithful to God, but he still had some growing to do. Especially frustrating was the fact that he had already been anointed by Samuel to be the next king. Now it looked as if he was likely to die. How long would he have to hide from Saul? How long would he be a fugitive? Where was God? The skies were silent.

While on the run, David was developing his military skills as well as learning to trust God completely. God needed a warrior king to lead Israel in victory. How could a shepherd boy know the ways of war? God's boot camp was a cave and a small group of recruits, and David was their general. In this divinely designed pressure situation, David would learn to manage men and to act according to God's timing. While David was waiting for God, God waited for David's growth.

Joseph dreamed of being placed in authority over others. He would be given that place for the purpose of saving the Messiah seed from starvation. But first he had to wait through a heart-wrenching placement process in Egypt and an unjust prison sentence to knock the rough edges off his arrogant spirit. God waited for the sake of Joseph's growth.

The key to the growth process is the patience to wait for God to work. Romans 5:3–4 claims, "We also rejoice in our sufferings, because we know that suffering produces perseverance; perseverance, character; and character, hope." James exhorts us to count it all joy because "you know that the testing of your faith develops perseverance. Perseverance must finish its work so that you may be mature and complete, not lacking anything" (James 1:2–4).

For a surgeon to do his good, yet painful work, the patient must lie still on the table. Anesthetic helps a lot! The anesthetic that stills our spirits during times of pressure and pain is knowing that God awaits our growth and is making us useful for His glory.

2. God waits for the sake of His glory.

In going through Genesis, we have already seen that God often chooses to wait until His people have moved into the arena of what they consider impossible. Then He acts so a watching world will know that He is the true and the living God, and so we will know firsthand the reality of His power on our behalf.

Why did God wait till Abraham and Sarah were past child-bearing age to give them a son? It was so He would be glorified and the credit would be totally His. Abraham and Sarah both needed firsthand experience with the glory of God. As faithful as they had been so far, neither of them really believed that He was the God of the impossible (Genesis 17:17–18; 18:10–14). Therefore, He allowed them to wait until it would take a miracle to honor His promise to them, and *then* He glorified Himself on their behalf.

When our oldest son, Joe, was small, Martie and I made a new covenant with God in regard to our finances. We reflected on the many times we had robbed God of the opportunity to provide by quickly exercising the power of our "plastic genie," and we claimed the promise of Philippians 4:19: "My God will meet all your needs according to his glorious riches in Christ Jesus." It wasn't long before the Lord tested our trust in His promise. An old Volkswagen was our only means of transportation. Its front right tire had worn bald, but we didn't have cash to buy a new one. Committing ourselves to claim God's promise and wait, one of us had the "bright" idea of including young Joe in the prayer effort. We wanted this to be a growth experience for him as well.

When we shared the need and asked him to pray with us, he respectfully replied, "Don't bother, Dad. God's too busy drinking Pepsi." You could have picked me up off the floor! Where did he ever get that idea? Then, it was as though the Holy Spirit speared me to the wall. We had taught him to pray, "Dear Heavenly Father," yet I was the only father he knew. I thought of the many times he had needed me and had asked for help, and I had replied with Pepsi in hand, "Not now, I'm too busy." I had diminished God's glory in my son's eyes! God is jealous that we know Him as He really is.

The next Sunday the financial secretary of our church handed me an envelope marked *Pastor Stowell and family*. We had told no one of our need, yet someone had placed that envelope in the offering plate with two new $20 bills inside. Forty dollars for our new tire. Forty dollars to prove to a young heart that God cares for the needs of His own. Forty dollars to show us His glory when all our options were gone! We were thankful we waited, because God showed Himself strong on our behalf.

3. *God waits because He works on our ground.*

God works His plans and purposes through our lives, our politics, our economics, our complexities, and Satan's domain. God's design is to work His will on our turf and in the environment of this world. That takes time because we are slow to change and Satan's domain is strong and aggressive. The Old Testament records a time when Daniel's prayer went unanswered for twenty one days because God's angel had been struggling with the demon that ruled the King of Persia (Daniel 10:1–3, 12–13). It is a credit to His character that God so patiently works with us on our turf to accomplish His plans.

God's time is always the right time. Periodically, my favorite baseball player goes into a batting slump. They say his timing is off. He is swinging ahead of the ball or behind the ball. The ball sets the standard. It crosses the plate at the right time. It's the hitter's responsibility to meet it there.

I can still remember how excited I was at the first birthday party my mom threw for me. I stood at the window and kept asking my mother, "When are they coming?" It wasn't yet time for my friends, but I couldn't wait. Eventually, after what seemed like an eternity, they began to arrive. They were right on time. When we press our faces to the window, waiting for God, we must believe that He will come right on time.

WE CAN WAIT WITH INTELLIGENT PATIENCE

As we learn to wait patiently for God to act, the first thing we must learn is that God has a purpose for delaying His response to us. That's *why* we wait. The second principle relates more to *how* we wait. It is beneficial and preferable for us to wait for God with *intelligent patience*.

Patience on our part must be more than the resolve of gritted teeth and well-meant commitment. Patience needs some handles we can hold on to. There are three.

Patience must first be filled with God's *promises*. God's Word has a promise for every crisis. Whether we need God's love, protection, grace, supply, wisdom, security, or comfort, penitence demands that we search the Bible for God's specific promise that relates to our dilemma. God is as good as His Word. He always keeps His promise in His time.

Second, patience must lay hold on God's *personality*. As we wait for Him, we can isolate a particular aspect of God's unfailing character and then depend on it. Whether it is His power, unconditional love, justice, holiness, wisdom, mercy, or truth, we must relate the appropriate aspect of His personality to each waiting experience.

Earlier we looked at David's agony while waiting in a cave for God to work. David resolved that wait by remembering that God loyally loves His own. David proclaimed, "I trust in your unfailing love; my heart rejoices in your salvation. I will sing to the Lord, for he has been good to me" (Psalm 13:5–6). Nothing had changed except that David had become patient by remembering that God is a God of unfailing love. Since God loyally loves us, we can wait for Him to act on our behalf.

Third, our patience must always be based on an awareness of the *principles* of God's Word. As we wait for God, it is often difficult to know how to act and what to do. Everything is permissible that doesn't violate God's principles. All our responses, attitudes, and actions need to be aligned with God's revealed will. Therefore, any revenge, murmuring, complaining, extended anger, hatred, and bitterness are clearly unwelcome as we wait. Genuine love toward others and submission to God's process must prevail. Often it will be challenging to know how to specifically respond. In those times, praying for wisdom (James 1:5) and seeking godly counsel (Proverbs 11:14) will be imperative.

The word *patience* in the New Testament is often the translation of a Greek word that literally means to "remain under" (Romans 5:3–4; Colossians 1:11; Hebrews 12:1). I am reminded of all the times my family has eaten a ripe, juicy watermelon. When we cut one open, one of us inevitably will press our thumb on a wet watermelon seed. You guessed it . . . out it shoots!

Christians often are like that. When pressure comes, we want to escape with the speed of a wet watermelon seed between thumb and forefinger. Yet patience is the virtue that provides the staying power to remain under the pressure of the situation in order to grow for God's glory as He works on our ground.

Our patience is energized by His promise and personality. It responds within the parameters of His principles. It is this kind of patience that protects us from Satan's temptations.

KINGDOM VICTORY WON

Because of the impatience of Abraham and Sarah, Satan's kingdom might have prevented the promised line of the Messiah. Ishmael would have been Abraham's only son. Isaac would never have been born. The genealogical line of Jesus would have come to an end almost as quickly as it had begun.

Yet once again, God theocratically intervened and overruled the forces of hell by rejecting Abraham's counterfeit seed (Genesis 17:17–19). He miraculously provided His seed, Isaac, through Sarah (21:1–17). God's victory is sure. The schemes of Satan will not prevail.

Mirrored in this aspect of the kingdom conflict is our vulnerability to impatience and the continuing consequences of our impatient choices. We need not fail. Indeed, our successful perseverance reflects God's strength and glory. As Paul wrote, "We pray this in order that you may live a life worthy of the Lord and may please him in every way: bearing fruit in every good work, growing in the knowledge of God, being strengthened with all power according to his glorious might *so that you may have great endurance and patience*, and joyfully giving thanks to the Father, who has qualified you to share in the inheritance of the saints in the kingdom of light" (Colossians 1:10–12, italics added).

Questions for Your Personal Conflict

1. When was the last time impatience (either yours or someone else's) got you in trouble or caused trouble for you?

2. Can you detect when you're becoming impatient, or do you only notice your impatience after you snap? How can you better control impatience before you do something you regret?

3. At what point do you think impatience moves from being a minor character flaw to becoming a significant spiritual problem?

4. In what ways might we tend to blame God as a result of being impatient toward someone else? How can impatience toward God be taken out on other people?

5. Which of the following areas of your life most need a healthy dose of renewed patience:
   ___ Work Life ___ Family Life
   ___ Relationships ___ Church Life
   ___ Prayer/Devotional Life ___ Other: _____

6. Read Isaiah 40:28–31. What are some of the benefits of patience in a spiritual context?

10

FOLLOWING ORDERS—
NO MATTER WHAT

Taking Obedience to a New Level

When you visit someone's home for the first time, it usually doesn't take long to determine what the person's priorities are. Photos are the logical first place to look. Whatever the person displays to see at regular intervals is usually something important to him or her. And there are other less obvious clues. Plastic on the furniture indicates a desire for neatness. A showcase full of tennis trophies and ribbons suggests the person is probably more than an occasional player. If the CD collection fills an entire wall, music is probably a passion for the person. And if you see youngsters with sticky fingers drinking grape juice on the white sofa, playing their favorite CDs, and dressing the people atop the tennis trophies in Barbie clothing, you joyfully discover that the children must certainly be a priority in the household.

We have an order to our lives similar to the order of our homes, and God is interested in knowing where He places in that order. Anything other than first place is less than He deserves. Less than He demands.

Throughout history, idolatry has been used effectively by Satan's kingdom to seduce us from our love relationship with Christ and His kingdom. At the heart of the issue of idolatry is determining who is first on the list of my loyalties. Who is my ultimate resource? For whom do I devote my life?

Most of us are too civilized to bow down to false gods of wood and stone, yet many of us carry on idolatrous affairs with houses, cars, relationships, bank accounts, or other accumulated things. All of these and more struggle to be first in our lives. Victory in the kingdom conflict demands persons who are committed to loving God more than anything else . . . persons who are able to give anything up should He require it . . . persons who are singleheartedly loyal to Christ. That's why Jesus pointed out that true discipleship is a matter of complete allegiance to Him (Luke 14:26–27).

It's important for us to sort out our priorities. We only discover our true condition when we are forced to make a choice. We can sing "I Surrender All" every morning for devotions and never know if we really mean it. But when we're faced with a choice that points to priorities, we finally see our true condition. Choices tell on us.

After being gone all week on business, will you spend Saturday playing golf with the guys, or at home with the family? Will you buy that new home entertainment center that you've always wanted, or funnel that money to the financial need of a friend? Will you spend your summer Sunday morning on your new boat, or faithfully worshiping God in the assembly of His people? Will you forgive the person who hurt you, or carry bitterness in your spirit? Loyalty is demonstrated in the crucible of choices.

GOD TESTS HIS PEOPLE

"This is a test. This is only a test." I've heard these words a hundred times, interrupting a program to test the emergency radio broadcast network. Still, I resent the annoying noise that follows and the wait, however short, until regular programming returns. I understand the need for tests, but I still don't enjoy them.

Of course, when I'm doing the testing, it's a different story. I've kicked my tires to test the pressure. I've knocked on wooden doors to see if they were solid or hollow. I've thumped on watermelons and pressed my fingers into apples to see if they were firm. I don't think twice about using pressure—even force—to test things and sense their true condition. In medieval times people used to test poets by placing them against a wall and hammering their foreheads. If no fractures resulted, the person was a true poet. (Now I know why my high school poetry classes were so hard to under-stand.)

It is not unusual for God to test His people. But His testing is always done in the context of His character and with a purpose. He tests us to reveal something to us and to a watching world. His tests not only reveal, but they also lead to reformation. As we see our-selves for what we are, we can willingly reposition ourselves before God.

When God tests us, He does so with a *careful hand*. He promis-es never to give us more than we can bear (1 Corinthians 10:13). If He tests us, we can be confident that it is at our level and within the scope of our ability to pass. There'll be no calculus tests for those of us in the second grade of Christian growth.

God also tests us with a *helping hand*. He promises that His grace, His help to us, is sufficient for any trial (2 Corinthians 12:9). I have often marveled as friends I love dearly have gone through tough tests. They've done so well. Because of their tests, I have seen the grace of God in action.

God most often tests us in the area of our priorities. On almost a daily basis we make choices that reveal where our loyalties lie. God gives us a multitude of opportunities to prove that He is Lord of our lives and not simply Lord of our lips.

As the kingdom conflict continues in the Genesis account, the promised messianic victory was threatened by misplaced alle-giance. After doing the impossible by giving Abraham and Sarah a son, God unexpectedly determined to test Abraham's loyalty. It was a most difficult test, a test in which Abraham would prove who placed first in his life.

PRIORITIES UNDER PRESSURE

God asked Abraham to take Isaac, his son, and sacrifice him on Mount Moriah (Genesis 22:2). Admittedly, this at first seems to be a cruel request that is out of character for God. But on more careful reflection, it is a perfectly designed test. In no other way could Abraham reveal that God held undisputed hold on first place in his life. There are two components to this test.

Emotional

The first component is emotional. We have a strong tendency to increase our love for the things God has given us while lessening our love for the Giver. Abraham loved Isaac deeply. This was his promised son, a miracle baby. Isaac was the next step in the promised line through Abraham. Isaac was the heir, the one and only child from his wife, Sarah. Though Abraham was a wealthy man, nothing was more beloved in his life than his precious son. How easy it would have been for Abraham to focus more intimately on Isaac, the gift, than on God, the Giver. When given a choice, would Abraham affirm his priority allegiance to God? Would he recognize that God was worthy to be his first love and to receive his unconditional allegiance?

Environmental

The second component in this test is environmental. Abraham had been placed as a sojourner in a pagan environment. For the Canaanites, the height of allegiance was the sacrificing of their children to their limp and lifeless gods. Would the one who was dedicated to the Almighty God have the depth of commitment that the pagans had? Did Abraham love his God as much?

What we give up for others is a compliment to their worth. When Martie and I were just beginning our ministry, dear friends came to visit us from out of state. We really couldn't afford it, but we wanted to make a statement of their worth to us and our love for them. That kind of statement required a sacrifice for us—prime rib dinner with all the trimmings as only Martie can fix. It was a financial stretch for us, but we considered it a statement of their worth.

Unfortunately, I sense that some Christians have categories of sacrifice for God. The Class "C" category includes all that we are glad to give up to prove our loyalty to Him—things like brussels sprouts, mowing the lawn, emptying the garbage, etc. We put up a bit more resistance to sacrifice things in the Class "B" list of allegiance, but if enough pressure comes from friends, sermons, or family members, we would probably put God before reading the daily paper and watching "Monday Night Football." It's the items in the Class "A" category of our lives that are often so hard to consider parting with. An unsaved boyfriend or girlfriend. A job. A child.

Fun and excitement. Money. Comfort. Pleasure. Hard-won positions in life. When God wants to test our priorities, He goes straight to the "A" list to see how we respond when He requests something of great significance to us. For Abraham, Isaac was at the top of his list in the Class "A" category.

GOD TESTS AT THE POINT OF SIGNIFICANCE

God was aware of how precious Isaac was to Abraham. Still, God told Abraham, "Take your son, your only son Isaac, whom you love" (Genesis 22:2). Note the threefold significance:

"*Your son*"—What could be closer to a parent's heart than one of his children? In Abraham's era, children were especially important since a childless home was an embarrassment and the children took care of the parents in their old age.

"*Your only son Isaac*"—Isaac was it. Ishmael had proven to be an illegitimate heir. Isaac was Abraham's singular possession. An only child is always special. This was certainly true for Abraham.

"Your only son Isaac, *whom you love*"—Just to remove any doubt, God acknowledges that He is aware of Abraham's love for Isaac. Of course Abraham loved the boy. He waited twenty-five years after God's original promise of an heir to see it fulfilled. Isaac was an everyday reminder that God does the impossible, having been born when Dad was one hundred and Mom was ninety. God was aware of all those feelings Abraham had for Isaac.

I'll never forget going to college as a freshman. It was my first fling with freedom, a new and exciting stage in life. My parents drove me there. They walked me through the registration process, and helped me unpack in my room. I met my roommate and it was instant friendship! I wanted to explore and meet new friends, so off I went with my roommate—and my Dad tagging along with us. I remember thinking, *Why does he stick around? I'm a college student now.*

At the end of the day, as Dad and Mom got in the car to go home, he wrote a check for the tuition payment and some spending money. As he tore it out of the checkbook and handed it to me, I noticed that his eyes were watered with tears. In a real sense his son, his only son, the son whom he loved, was gone! I've wished a thousand times that I could have that moment and that day back again to tell him how much I really loved and appreciated him. It was a time of separation. That must be in small measure some of what Abraham felt as God required his son.

One Saturday night at 11 A.M. I awoke to the sound of my phone ringing. The urgent voice on the other end told me of a horrible auto accident that had just taken place. One car had burst into flames and the other was demolished. The demolished car belonged to my friends Dave and Debbie. Their only child, Shawn, had been with them. I called the hospital and told them I was their pastor. The hospital spokesman said, "If you're their minister, you should come here right away."

As I walked by the cubicles in the emergency room, I saw several doctors and nurses working feverishly over Shawn, who was soon to slip out of this life. Dave was in a restless coma and Debbie was in shock, with deep and extensive cuts on her face from the broken windshield. It took hours of surgery to restore Debbie to some semblance of herself. The family asked me to stay through the night and relate the news to Debbie about Shawn. It was well into Sunday morning before Debbie was in a condition to ask about her son. All I could tell her was that he had gone to a better place—he was now in the arms of Jesus.

That was a hard loss. God had required their son, their only son, the son whom they loved. Think of how difficult this was for Abraham. God was requiring the same thing, only Abraham would have a choice. If the choice were yours, what would you say to God?

GOD'S TESTS SEEMINGLY CONFLICT WITH HIS PROMISES

It seems that what God asked Abraham to do makes no sense at all. Isaac was the promised son, the one designated to carry on the victory line. Why would God require the very thing He had promised and provided?

Our possessions often become sources of our security, peace, joy, and confidence. We have come to expect God to provide fulfillment through the *things* He has given us. When obedience to Him requires giving up something of significance, it seems to conflict with His promises of security, peace, and joy.

My friend Jerry made a sacrificial financial contribution to support the eternal work of Christ's kingdom. His confidence was in God's promise to supply his needs, and rightly so (Philippians 4:10–19). Yet the very next day he received a letter from the city informing him of a zoning ordinance requiring him to pave the parking lot of his business. It didn't make sense. The paving would cost a lot of money. What God required didn't square with what God had promised.

Yet even though God's requirement from Abraham was going to be his only son, Abraham obeyed. The command of God was clear. Abraham would prove that God was his top priority—regardless.

If we try to put ourselves in Abraham's place, we cringe at the thought. We wonder how a loving father could ever plunge a knife into the child that he loves. But what we don't understand is the level of faith that Abraham had in his God. His faith allowed him to believe in the supernatural ability of God to keep His promise in spite of His requirements:

> By faith Abraham, when God tested him, offered Isaac as a sacrifice. He who had received the promises was about to sacrifice his one and only son, even though God had said to him, "It is through Isaac that your offspring will be reckoned." Abraham reasoned that God could raise the dead, and figuratively speaking, he did receive Isaac back from death. (Hebrews 11:17–19)

WHEN GOD REQUIRES, GOD REPAYS

When God requires from us what He has promised to us, He always—eventually, supernaturally—repays. And when He does, we are better off than before. Abraham was able to obey because he knew God could not be unfaithful to Himself. Since God could not give up His faithfulness, Abraham could give up his son. Abraham saw his sacrifice in the light of the One he was sacrificing to. He demonstrated that his security in life lay not in possessions, but rather in his God; not in the gift, but in the Giver.

God must keep His promises. If He requires something He has promised to us, the loss will only be temporary. My friend Jerry went ahead and had his parking lot paved. It was a tremendous expense that drained his capital. Yet several months later he excitedly related that since paving the lot, his business had increased far beyond the paving expenses. I thought to myself, *When God requires, God repays.* He doesn't always respond *when* we think He should or *the way* we think He should, but He always repays in His time . . . and in better currency.

Our friends Tim and Barbara dated throughout college. They both loved the Lord and were making plans to go into missions together. In the spring of their senior year, after four years of "open season" on potential mates was almost over, Tim changed his mind about missions and decided to pursue a church ministry instead. Barbara knew the foreign field was where she was best suited to serve her Lord. She held to her resolve. Not only was God requiring her marriage, dreams, and new home—He was also expecting her to go it alone through the difficulties of deputation and cultural adjustment. Yet God had undisputed first place in her life. She sacrificed all she had on her own Mount Moriah and went to Brazil. I watched with a deep sense of admiration. Several years later, we received a letter from Barbara rejoicing in the fact that she had met a dynamic missionary who happened to be a widower. They fell in love, married and—you guessed it—instant family! Who would have ever expected God to repay so dramatically?

God does not always respond as quickly or as obviously as He did for Jerry and for Barbara. Often He repays in quieter, more long-range ways. But we can always depend on Him to keep His promises. Our faith in His faithfulness, even though it might be displayed in supernatural ways, releases us to place Him in undiminished first place in our lives—with *nothing* between our souls and the Savior. The songwriter put it this way:

> Modern times have brought us many comforts,
> People live in wealth and luxury;
> But the Master still asks this question,
> "Lovest thou Me, Lovest thou Me more than these?"
> "Lovest thou Me more than these, My child?
> What will your answer be?"
> "O precious Lord, I love Thee more than all of these—
> More than fame,
> More than wealth,
> More than the world."

ABRAHAM MEANT IT

Perhaps the most amazing aspect of the account of Abraham and Isaac is that Abraham did not know this was only a test. When he said yes to God, he meant it. He obeyed because God was first in his life, and he would have obeyed completely. He knew that God would repay supernaturally if necessary. It is the mark of a true friend of God to be unflinchingly loyal to Him.

As Abraham demonstrated this unquestioning commitment, God stopped the test and said, "Abraham! Abraham! . . . Do not lay a hand on the boy . . . Do not do anything to him. Now I know that you fear God, because you have not withheld from me your son, your only son" (Genesis 22:11–12). After revealing some previous failures and shortcomings in regard to Sarah, Abraham passed this test with flying colors. He learned the joy of full and complete obedience.

God then resumed the normal programming of the kingdom victory. Abraham had proved something to God, and something to himself. He would never be the same again.

Is there anything you wouldn't give up for God?

An honest answer to that question determines where God places in your priorities.

Questions for Your Personal Conflict

1. If someone saw your house for the first time, what would he or she suppose your top priorities are? If someone observed your words and actions for a week, what priorities do you think the person would assume you have?

2. What was the hardest thing God has ever asked or expected you to do?

3. How do you feel when you're put to a spiritual test? What do you think is an appropriate amount of testing for a participant in the kingdom conflict?

4. How does "passing" a test of God make you feel? What lasting benefits do you receive? What effect does it have on others around you?

5. Read Judges 6–7. From these stories of Gideon, what additional things can you learn about being tested and relying on God during difficult times?

11

CONFLICT WITHIN THE RANKS
The Battle Against Immediate Gratification

Vandals sneaked into a hardware store one night. But rather than steal anything or destroy the merchandise, they left everything in order—except for switching around all the price tags. As customers arrived the next morning they found that nails were $2.99 apiece, televisions 79¢ per pound, hammers $499.95 with remote control, and screwdrivers $24.99. Much confusion resulted as shoppers lost all perspective regarding the true value of things.

Values. Living on the conquering edge in the kingdom conflict demands that we assign appropriate worth to matters of now and eternity. Think of the showroom of your life. You determine the value of items such as cars, houses, lost souls, wardrobes, Christ's kingdom work, vacations, money, missions, the poor, friends, and food. All these things carry tags upon which you mark their worth. How you mark them reflects what you value most.

Everything begins with values. Values determine our choices, and choices determine our destinies—destinies of joy and freedom or sorrow and regret.

How can we discern true values? Christ clearly established a standard of worth, a standard that cuts across the mismatched values of our world. When a man asked Jesus to demand that his brother share an inheritance with him, He countered the man's covetousness with the profound statement, "Watch out! Be on your guard against all kinds of greed; a man's life does not consist in the abundance of his possessions" (Luke 12:15).

Jesus went on to demonstrate that eternal life was of far greater value than riches and success (Luke 12:16–21; Matthew 16:26). He taught that the principles and programs of God's kingdom were more important than even the basics of life (Luke 12:22–32). He acknowledged the value of money as being useful in His service while warning against the bankruptcy that results from using money to satisfy ourselves (Luke 16:9–13).

And what of eternal gain? Christ said that its value was incomparably higher than giving our lives for the things "moth and rust destroy, and . . . thieves break in and steal" (Matthew 6:19). If you value the things of the world too highly, it is then impossible to love the Father (Luke 16:13; 1 John 2:15–17). We are to place supreme value on God and His will for us. The Bible is quite specific in the area of values clarification.

Scripture never advises that we should own nothing and desire nothing. That is not the point. The point of Scripture is that whatever we own and whatever we want must be appropriately tagged. God, His will for us, and matters of eternity must be marked as treasures never to be sold, the priceless commodities of our lives tagged "Not for sale. Non-negotiable."

The things of this earth, on the other hand, are to be used for God's glory. We should consider them expendable, subject to the Father's will, transferable to kingdom currency, tools for servanthood.

The issue of values is not a matter of what we own, but rather a matter of what owns us. The truth of Scripture affirms that we are owned by the Father who bought us with a price (1 Corinthians 6:20). He rescued us from the slave block in the marketplace of sin. We should now freely serve our new and gracious Master, rather than the things of this world or the ways of the system.

Yet the competition is strong. The gravity of things tugging on the desire strings of our hearts keeps the issue fresh before us. Tagging the merchandise of our lives by kingdom standards—and then making sure the tags don't get switched—is the only way to overcome this gravity of the flesh.

MISTAGGED LIVES

As the kingdom conflict continues in the book of Genesis, Satan uses the tactic of misplaced values to attack the promised kingdom of Christ. In this case, his target is Esau. As the firstborn, Esau was the natural successor to the promise of Genesis 3:15, and could possibly have been the fulfillment of it. His birthright entitled him to precedence over other children in the family and a double share of his father's inheritance. Yet in a moment of escalated desire, he lost track of the value of what he possessed. He became vulnerable to a scheme by Jacob that would rob him and leave him with an irreplaceable loss. At a more significant level, Esau left himself open to yet another scheme of Satan to displace the Messiah promise and frustrate the plan of God.

The story is told in Genesis 25:29–34. After a hard day out in the country, Esau was famished when he returned home. Jacob happened to be cooking some stew and saw an opportunity to strike a bargain. Sure enough, Esau valued lunch more than his birthright, and he sold it to Jacob in exchange for a hearty meal.

Esau's response in this situation is instructive. When our values are threatened like his were, there is a specific pattern. First comes the *hunger.* Desires will always live within us. Desires are not wrong in themselves, but they can become handles for Satan's manipulation. We hunger for happiness, wealth, possessions, prestige, recognition, beauty, sensual fulfillment, comfort, friends, and even food. These are the items that become the "lunches" for which we are tempted to trade our spiritual birthright. In the face of these desires, we must remember that our birthright guarantees that we have all we need in and from God. (See Ephesians 1:3–14; Philippians 4:13, 19; and Hebrews 13:5–6.) There is never a need or desire we should value more highly than the Savior.

Susan accepted Christ at a women's Bible study. Like many new believers, she zealously began to study the Scriptures. Her husband, however, became increasingly upset with his wife's newfound faith. He would come home to find her reading the Bible and would coerce her to get her to stop, but to no avail. Finally, in desperation, he presented a substitute. "Susan," he said, "I will buy you a fur coat; in fact, I will even buy you a new car. I'm willing to buy you whatever you desire if you will just give up that Bible." Her answer was from the heart. "Greg, you've provided me with a home and family and children. I just don't need any of those other things. I'm happy with what I have." At that point Greg realized that his wife possessed something he lacked. He knew too that he wanted it. In the quietness of his family room he accepted the Savior into his life as Susan had done earlier.

We, like Esau, have to deal with our hungers. But the second issue we see from Esau's life is an *attitude* problem. Scripture tells us he despised his birthright (Genesis 25:34).

It's not difficult to have the wrong attitude toward spiritual things. Things of the kingdom are usually unseen and long-range. Many of us never develop a genuine appreciation for spiritual values. This is especially true of second- and third-generation believers who tend to hitchhike on their heritages. They consider themselves Christians because they grow up in a Christian family, yet they never experience spiritual reality firsthand. Their attitudes toward spiritual things are never what they ought to be. Consequently, their entire value system becomes distorted.

Third, Esau had to make a *sacrifice* in order to find any kind of satisfaction. He felt the hunger, and he had the wrong attitude toward spiritual things. Consequently, he sacrificed something he *should* have valued just to feed his hunger.

A sure signal that we are failing in the matter of values is when we sacrifice something of true value to satisfy our desires. When someone enters a value crisis without a developed sense of priority love for the kingdom, it becomes easy to sacrifice what is truly meaningful in exchange for something of far less value. It may be the sacrifice of one's testimony, financial freedom, clear conscience, family atmosphere, moral strength and purity, positive relationships, communication with the Holy Spirit, or even the strength and health of one's body.

Fourth, Esau *traded a short-term gain for a long-term loss*. Things of the kingdom are usually unseen and long-range. We are told to expect rewards for them, but the payoff doesn't come for a long while. When I was just beginning ministry, a wise friend told me that spiritual maturity was measured by a person's willingness to take a short-term loss for a long-term gain. The same measurement should be used when determining right values. People loyal to the values of the kingdom refuse to barter the eternal in the market-place of the immediate. On the other hand, persons intent on quick rewards will continually experience loss of long-term rewards such as family, spiritual growth, prayer, witness, and continued faithfulness.

Esau is only one of many biblical illustrations of mistagged values. A New Testament example is the rich ruler who came to Christ wanting to know how he might inherit eternal life (Luke 18:18–23). Jesus' response immediately brought the ruler's sense of values to the surface: "Sell everything you have and give to the poor, and you will have treasure in heaven. Then come, follow me." Jesus was not saying that you could be saved by giving everything you own to the poor. Rather, He was speaking to this one specific wealthy man, weighing the value of eternal life against the other possessions in his heart. Eternal life must be received unconditionally and esteemed as a top priority. The rich man left sorrowfully (Luke 18:23) because he wasn't ready to value the kingdom more than his cash and possessions. Many follow in his footsteps. When people refuse to come to Christ because of what they might have to give up to be a disciple, their choice reflects what they value most in life.

Judas is another example of misplaced values. It seems hard to believe, but he valued thirty pieces of silver more than his relationship with his friend and teacher, the Messiah. Judas is noteworthy because he was one of the inner circle. He claimed commitment to Christ, yet betrayed Him when the chips were down. When I look at Judas, I am faced with a frightening truth, *If he was vulnerable to a crisis in values, certainly I too could betray Christ with misplaced values.* What was it in Judas' life that so disoriented his sense of what was right?

In contrast is Mary's grateful gift of worship to Christ (John 12:1–8). She anointed Jesus with a pound of spikenard—an expensive, prized perfume worth approximately a year's wages. Its worth to her personally would be measured in the status of having so much of that kind of prestigious perfume. Did you ever notice how women display their perfume fragrances on their dressers? I'm not sure what other varieties Mary had—"My Sin," "Midnight in Moab"—who knows? But she did have a pound of spikenard. Jesus had just raised her brother, Lazarus, from the dead (John 11). How could she say thanks? How could she express His value to her? By giving to Him her prized possession in an act of worship. She had her values straight.

As she poured it over Jesus' feet, Judas asked, "Why wasn't this perfume sold and the money given to the poor?" (John 12:5). He sounded like a man with solid values. But the text parenthetically informs us of the true condition of his heart. John says that Judas really didn't value the poor, but rather was a thief. As the treasurer for the disciples, Judas carried the moneybag and stole from it for himself (John 12:6). His commitment was not to Christ, but to cash. He valued personal gain above the gain of the kingdom. Therefore, when the right opportunity came along, it was easy for him to betray Christ.

I'm convinced that when Judas realized that Jesus was going to the cross, when he realized that his dreams of being the treasurer of the messianic kingdom on earth had crumbled, when his vision of personal riches had burst, then the thirty pieces of silver loomed as the best offer he could get out of the deal. Enter betrayal!

For Judas, Christ had been simply a means to an end. He valued Jesus only as long as it was beneficial to his personal plans. He was betrayal looking for a place to happen. Unlike the rich ruler who stayed outside the kingdom because of his mistagged values, Judas was a phony living inside the kingdom.

How easy it is to be like Judas. Outwardly we confess kingdom values, yet inwardly we devote ourselves to the values of the world. We detect signs of our divided loyalties when we are willing to exchange character for cash, conviction for convenience, Christ for comfort, purity for pleasure, holiness for self-fulfillment, financial faithfulness for material gain, God's way for our way, or truth for error. Each of these actions is a betrayal kiss on the cheek of Christ who dwells within us.

In the perspective of the kingdom conflict, it becomes clear that warped values are effective weapons in Satan's arsenal against God. Not only did Satan exercise this tactic through Esau at the beginning of the Messiah line (Genesis 25), but it was his best shot when he wanted to pull off an inside job to nail the Messiah to the cross. It is sobering to realize how destructive warped values can be—today as much as ever.

Martie and I were invited to a friend's home to meet Bob and his wife. We drove down the wooded driveway and noticed Bob's beautiful luxury car outside the house. Bob wasn't yet thirty, but he was obviously successful. As we sat and talked, Bob began to unfold the story of his life. He had left home to go to college, but soon dropped out to pursue "the good life." Then one day he looked at himself and heard the words his father had used so many times, *Bob, you're nothing but a bum*. Bent on proving his father wrong, Bob returned to his home state and opened a business that soon became a great success.

He married and bought an estate in the country with horses and acreage. He had everything he'd ever dreamed of and more. But while talking with us, Bob said several times, "After I had all I wanted, I felt empty and frustrated." Personal fulfillment had become the only thing he could not buy. As a result, he had seriously contemplated suicide on more than one occasion.

Bob had learned early in life that the quick rewards of this world bring only momentary pleasure with no in-depth, long-term gain. Valuing the things of this world's system is like trying to carry water in a bucket full of holes. No matter how hard we try or how often we fill the bucket, it soon is empty again.

After Esau's stew was eaten, he would soon be hungry again. The rich ruler walked away from Jesus without eternal life. Judas's thirty pieces of silver would quickly lose their value in his hand. Bob's "everything" was really nothing.

A SORRY STATE

Proverbs 10:22 teaches us, "The blessing of the Lord brings wealth, and he adds no trouble to it." The King James Version translates the word "trouble" as *sorrow*. When God is our top priority, we can have blessing without sorrow. Those who sacrifice true values for the false values of this world may get what they want to some degree, yet they are almost always left with the residue of regret.

Esau wept with great sorrow when he realized what he had lost

(Genesis 27:34; Hebrews 12:17). The ruler who came to Christ went away with sorrow in his heart (Luke 18:23–24). Judas too felt the sorrow of misplaced values (Matthew 27:1–5).

For us, the sorrow of misplaced values is felt in many different ways: relationships that are irretrievably broken, guilt, children who refuse to share our faith, worry and anxiety in the area of finances, and looking back over one's life and seeing nothing of significance, only the litter of shallow choices. We make many choices that seem so right, so fulfilling, yet which ultimately bring emptiness and sorrow. As we reflect on past decisions to pursue the things of this world at the expense of things of true value, sorrow is a natural byproduct. Both Esau's and Judas's lives pointedly exemplify the types of sorrow that Satan pays as his ultimate dividend. Let's take a closer look.

Sorrow of the Irretrievable

Esau's sorrow centered in the fact that his choice had caused him to lose something he could never gain again (Hebrews 12:16–17). How often do we look backward and think: *If only I had that day to live over again*, or *If only I had stopped before saying that?* But once the word has been said or the action taken, it is sometimes too late to undo the damage. The previous relationship is irretrievable.

Scientists have studied the genetic structure of lizards to see if somehow humans might ever be able to grow back lost arms and legs like certain reptiles do. Whether or not the scientists will be successful, one thing is sure—our lives are not like lizards' legs. Our misplaced values often leave us as emotional or spiritual amputees.

Sorrow of Lingering Anger and Bitterness

Esau responded to Jacob's devious and manipulative action with great anger and a lingering bitterness (Genesis 27:41). When our values are misplaced, we are always vulnerable to be taken advantage of by others. We do things we know to be unethical "because it's my job." We buy things for status or show, rather than living within our means. We even do things willingly "for the sake of friendship" that we wouldn't do otherwise. And later, *even though we chose to take those actions*, we feel angry and bitter toward the other people involved.

A person will often become angry with a sexual partner who "took advantage" of him or her and then never called again. In the reality of "the morning after," the person can't deny having made the choice to become sexually active. Yet while in a vulnerable state, the person is used by another because his or her values are established not on an unflinching commitment to Christ, but on security, self-fulfillment, and peer acceptance. How natural to then lash back at the one who had taken advantage of a poor value system. Lingering anger only compounds our sorrow.

Sorrow of Seeing

Hindsight usually gives us a much more accurate view of our value choices. When Judas saw what happened to Jesus as a result of what he had done, sorrow entered his heart (Matthew 27:3). Like Judas, when we choose things of lesser value and betray what is really important in life, we may become suddenly aware of the consequences of our decisions.

Parents who have neglected the importance of their home often see, too late, the sorrowful results of their choices in the actions and attitudes of their children. Some who have chosen lucrative careers over service-oriented vocations reflect with sorrow over "what might have been." Some who rejected wise advice and chose wrong marriage partners experience continuing sorrow because of their decisions. When it comes to a false system of values, what you see at the outset is not what you get in the final analysis.

Sorrow of Symbols

My dad would often tell me, "Joe, the trouble with you is that money burns a hole in your pocket." For Judas, his thirty pieces of silver burned a hole in his heart. We are told that after he saw that Jesus had been condemned, he returned to the chief priests and elders, throwing the money back at them (Matthew 27:3–5). Why? Because the money had become symbolic of his sorrow. The silver reminded him of what he had done to Christ as a result of his faulty value system.

I was the pastor of a church that undertook a building project. The decorating committee had worked very hard and had determined to carpet the entire office complex in earth tones. My secretary, however, dared to be different. She asked for blue in her office, and she prevailed. But the day before the decision was finalized, she told me that she had changed her mind and would have earth tones like everyone else. I was surprised. She had been the only one with the courage to disagree with the decorating committee. She explained that she realized the blue carpeting would only be a symbol of her stubbornness, and had decided she didn't want a daily reminder.

I must confess that I am an unrepentant "lawn-aholic." If I had time, I would probably measure and cut each blade of grass individually. As a result, I spend much of my spare time manicuring our yard. My son has a similar passion for basketball. Many times he has invited me to come play with him, only to have me turn him down because I was doing yard work. In fact, I would sometimes explain that he should come and help *me* with the lawn. After all, yard work builds character!

As I got home one afternoon after visiting a family whose child was tragically ill, I noticed how good my yard looked. For once, the grass was not greener on the other side of the fence. I turned into my driveway feeling really good about myself, only to see the basketball hoop at the other end. When I saw it, my mind replayed the events of the afternoon, and I thought about my son and how thankful I was to come home to a healthy boy. As I looked at the grass, it suddenly represented my failure to spend time with my son, to meet him on his level. I knew then that if it had been my son in the hospital, I would have hated my grass that day and longed for a moment of basketball in the driveway with my son. What was once my joy had become a symbol of sorrow. I opened the door and yelled, "Hey, Joe, let's play basketball." To my amusement, he replied, "Not now, Dad, I'm busy." But from that point on, I was more aware of how much time I spent doing what *he* liked to do.

Sorrow of Suicide

Sorrow is a powerful emotion. When it is mixed with guilt, as in cases where we look back over our wrong decisions and misplaced values, the results are occasionally deadly. The Chicago newspapers recently picked up a story from Pennsylvania about a motorcyclist who accidentally hit and killed a six-year-old girl riding her bicycle. The twenty-five-year-old man had apparently been going pretty fast at the time. Witnesses explained that when he saw what he had done, he began crying and yelling, "Forgive me! Forgive me!" Then he walked to the side of the road, pulled a pistol out of his pocket, and shot and killed himself. The man had a steady job, a permit for the gun, and no criminal record. But apparently he felt that he could not live with his sorrow.

In the kingdom conflict, where spiritual issues and eternal consequences are at stake, the sorrow we feel after our failures can be quite severe. To make things worse, Satan seeks to destroy us (1 Peter 5:8). He will do everything in his power to use and manipulate us, but as soon as we attempt to repent or rectify past sins, he will turn on us without mercy. Judas was so empty and sorrowful that he went out and hanged himself (Matthew 27:5). His value choice had left his bucket empty. Satan always wastes his heroes.

Judas's action reminds me of Paul's commentary on values:

> Godliness with contentment is great gain. For we brought nothing into the world, and we can take nothing out of it. But if we have food and clothing, we will be content with that. People who want to get rich fall into temptation and a trap and into many foolish and harmful desires that plunge men into ruin and destruction. For the love of money is a root of all kinds of evil. Some people, eager for money, have wandered from the faith and pierced themselves with many griefs. (1 Timothy 6:6–10)

All of us make mistakes in life, and it is inevitable that our mistakes will cause sorrow at some point. When we encounter such times, we must always remember that we serve a God of love and forgiveness. Satan wants to take us down with him. God wants to lift us up. Yes, we might have to live with the consequences of past mistakes, yet God in His mercy can make those things bearable. Sorrow need not consume us. With God, there is always help and hope.

Earlier in the chapter I told you about Bob, a businessman who discovered that money couldn't buy happiness. But I didn't tell you the whole story. As Bob continued telling Martie and me about his life, he explained how furious he had become when his wife received Christ. He let her know he thought religion was only for weak people—blind, lame, or sick. Yet within him was a gnawing emptiness that got worse as he watched his wife's life become filled with the reality of Christ. One day on a business trip, alone in a motel room, Bob knelt and asked God to save him. He told us, "Since I met Christ and have learned to walk with Him, I am the happiest I have ever been in my life." Bob had clarified his values, and the blessings of the Lord had made him rich—with no sorrow!

GOD'S KINGDOM VICTORY

Because of Esau's ill-advised trade, his birthright was now in the hand of one who was not the intended heir (Genesis 27), yet God would theocratically guarantee the victory promise. Esau was not worthy of it; he had despised and devalued it. Jacob had desired it, even though he sought it wrongfully. God would now pass the promise to Jacob (28:13–15) and refine Jacob's manipulative, self-sufficient attitude through a crisis at Laban's house (29:1–30) and a supernatural wrestling match (32:23–30).

In one of the most moving scenes in Genesis, Esau eventually forgave Jacob when he could have killed him (33:1–4). That was significant. His forgiveness preserved the Messiah seed for God's kingdom victory. It's never too late to play a part for God!

Once more God intervened to sovereignly assure His promise. Though Esau forfeited God's blessing by valuing a pot of stew more than the promise of God, the seed of the Messiah was left intact.

Questions for Your Personal Conflict

1. Have you ever beaten someone out of something—either fair-and-square or somewhat deceitfully—only to regret it later? What changed your mind? How did you resolve the situation?

2. How do you feel when someone else gets something that by all rights should be yours? How do you tend to respond in such cases?

3. We experience problems when we accept a long-term loss in order to have short-term gains. Can you reverse the process by identifying some potential short-term gains you would be willing to sacrifice to ensure a more lasting long-term benefit? (Be as specific as possible.)

4. What sorrows are you currently dealing with? Based on what you have read in this chapter, how do you think you should proceed from this point?

5. Read Genesis 27–35. While this chapter has focused on the lessons that Esau learned, we can also learn much from the story of Jacob that follows. As you read the narrative, compile a list of lessons and/or principles you can apply to your own life.

12

SUCCESS BEHIND ENEMY LINES
The Battle Against Discouragement

An old folk tale tells of Satan auctioning off his tools. All but one were for sale. A potential buyer looked carefully at the hooked instrument and asked what it was for. Satan replied, "I can spare any other tool, but I cannot spare this one. It is the most useful implement I have. It is called discouragement, and with it I can work my way into hearts otherwise inaccessible."

Discouragement disables us from the inside out. All of us have felt it. It is the wilting of our hearts, a certain sense of defeat. Discouragement is the prelude to despair. It opens the doors to depression, self-pity, negative thinking, withdrawal, and a host of other destructive influences.

While God never promises that discouraging circumstances won't come our way, He does provide the means by which we can shield our hearts from debilitating discouragement. He desires that we live graciously and powerfully in the midst of our circumstances. I have a special admiration for people who rise from the depths of discouragement and go on with their lives. That's why I appreciate the account of Joseph and find myself captivated by his life story.

THE TROUBLE WITH RIGHTEOUSNESS

The life history of Joseph begins with the observation that he did not share in the evil of his brothers (Genesis 37:2). Joseph had a bent toward righteousness. That makes everything that happens to him more intriguing. Joseph is about to be displaced from his family and deserted unjustly in a foreign jail. In each instance, it is his righteousness that induces the crisis.

The quicker we get over the notion that righteousness guarantees a trouble-free life, the better equipped we will be to persevere and stand victorious in the conflict. Righteousness, in fact, often creates a crisis because we live in the unrighteous domain of Satan. We swim upstream. That creates the friction of conviction in the lives of unrighteous people who will in turn seek to create trouble for the source of their conviction. The most righteous Man who ever lived suffered at the hands of the unrighteous and warned His followers that they would experience the same kind of treatment (John 15:18–27).

In fact, it is in crisis situations that we grow spiritually. God assures us that He uses our crises to refine us. Paul describes the process: "We also rejoice in our sufferings, because we know that suffering produces perseverance; perseverance, character; and character, hope. And hope does not disappoint us, because God has poured out his love into our hearts by the Holy Spirit, whom he has given us" (Romans 5:3–5). James reiterates this theme when he exhorts us to "consider it pure joy, my brothers, whenever you face trials of many kinds, because you know that the testing of your faith develops perseverance. Perseverance must finish its work so that you may be mature and complete, not lacking anything" (James 1:2–4).

Our sufferings result in spiritual growth, and that growth equips us to be useful for God's glory. God is always stretching us toward greater effectiveness. We are in process. Part of that process includes growing in the midst of pain—pain that is sometimes the result of righteousness.

As we look at the life of Joseph, note that in all his trouble the pattern is clear: (1) his commitment to righteousness; (2) trouble as a result of the commitment; (3) refinement as a consequence of the trouble; and (4) great usefulness for the kingdom and purposes of God.

SATAN'S STRATEGY

When we examine Joseph's life in the extraterrestrial dimension of the kingdom conflict, we see that he qualifies to be the chief concern of the kingdom of Satan. His father Jacob (Israel) had received the promise of the Messiah (Genesis 28:13–15). Jacob had twelve sons, but only one stood out as righteous—the one who could well be the inheritor of the victory promise (Genesis 3:15). In response, Satan engineered a process that would isolate this potential Messiah seed from his family and leave him deserted in a foreign jail.

Satan's strategy was twofold. First, Satan *displaced* Joseph from family and inheritance and isolated him in a foreign land. Second, Satan placed Joseph in a setting ripe for *discouragement* and the development of bitterness and hatred. If Joseph had given in to the bitterness, Satan's plan might have succeeded in interfering with the promise through the line of Jacob's sons (Genesis 50:15–21).

DISPLACED PERSONS

Several years ago the chief executive of Holiday Inns resigned because the Board of Directors voted to open a gambling casino in their hotel chain. The man found himself displaced from his high-level job because of his righteousness. Yet God was able to use his displacement. His name, previously obscure in connection with Christ's kingdom, was suddenly placed in a conspicuous place of testimony and outreach. Newspapers carried his story, and he since has had high visibility for the kingdom work of Christ. Suffering displacement because of righteousness works as God's placement service to put us in the right spot to be useful and effective.

Daniel and his friends are biblical examples of this truth. Shadrach, Meshach, Abednego, and Daniel found themselves displaced *geographically* from their homeland and deposited in the pagan land of Babylon. There they found themselves displaced *spiritually* because of their righteousness. Daniel's steadfast righteousness landed him in the lions' den. Shadrach, Meshach, and Abednego were tossed into the fiery furnace for similar reasons. But God protected them. Both times the secular world rulers were confronted

with the awesome power of the true and living God, and His faithful people came out better off than they were before. Christ
Himself, our model of righteousness, was displaced into a tomb only
to be repositioned right where He would prove to a watching world
that He was the supreme victor over death and hell.

A high school girl complained to me that her parents were too
restrictive. Among other things, they were refusing to let her go to a
party Friday night that all her friends planned to attend. Didn't her
parents trust her? After all, she wasn't a child anymore! She dis-
agreed with their decision, and it was tough, but she obeyed. She
displayed righteousness in action. The following Sunday she told
me she'd heard that some of the guests at the party had brought
drugs. As the alcohol flowed, the party got loud and wild. Neighbors
called the police and some of the kids were even arrested. As she
related the events of this evening to me, I could tell my young
friend was thrilled that her obedience had displaced her from the
party that night.

When we are righteously displaced, God repositions us where
He will either use us or protect us. Such was the case with Joseph.

QUALITY RIGHTEOUSNESS

A commitment to righteousness charts a clear course. It dic-
tates behavior and direction in life. Joseph was a young man
uniquely committed to righteousness, and in that commitment
there was a price to pay.

I am intrigued by the quality of Joseph's righteousness. It is put
to the test three times. His righteousness was exercised in the context of: (1) his father's intentions; (2) moral purity; and (3) forgiveness.

In the first instance, Joseph's father told him, "As you know,
your brothers are grazing the flocks near Shechem. Come, I am
going to send you to them" (Genesis 37:13). Joseph was instructed
to check on the welfare of the brothers who hated him. It would be
no picnic, but he obeyed.

The extent of Joseph's righteousness is seen in the decision he
made after he got to Shechem. The brothers weren't there. Joseph
could have gone home and told his father in all honesty that he had

tried, but couldn't find his brothers. Yet amazingly enough, Joseph obeyed not only his father's words, but also his father's intentions. His father wanted him to check on his brothers' welfare, so Joseph finally tracked them down in Dothan. That's quality righteousness. Joseph went the extra mile—several extra miles, as a matter of fact. And what was the reward for his righteousness? His brothers decided, "This is the opportunity we've been looking for to get rid of little brother. We'll sell the brat and never have to see him again!" Joseph was displaced by quality righteousness—all the way to Egypt.

While in Egypt, Joseph became the trusted manager of Potiphar's household. Away from family influence and rejected by his brothers, Joseph was totally on his own, but still he remained faithful to God. His next test came when Potiphar's wife attempted to seduce him . . . day after day (Genesis 39:7). Joseph always refused her advances. Finally, in desperation, Potiphar's wife made a grab for Joseph. He escaped and fled, leaving his robe behind (39:10–12).

Joseph demonstrated his righteousness through his moral purity. He was a young man, alone and rejected. A beautiful Egyptian woman tried to seduce him daily. No one would ever know if he had given in to her. Yet Joseph knew that such an action would be offensive to God (39:9), and he stood firm. The result was a false accusation of attempted rape and an undeserved prison sentence. Joseph was displaced again.

In the closing chapter of Genesis, Joseph has persevered and is now second to Pharaoh in authority over all of Egypt. His brothers, who previously rejected him and sold him into slavery, stand before him (50:15–21). They are at his mercy and fear for their lives. Here was Joseph's opportunity to pay them back for their rejection, hatred, and all he had suffered because of what they did to him. But Joseph once again demonstrated righteousness. He forgave them. He could see that his being sold into slavery was only the first of a long and unusual chain of events—frequently unpleasant events—that God strung together to make sure Joseph was in God's place at a crucial time. And thanks to Joseph's righteousness and forgiveness, the promised Messiah seed was spared from extermination.

DISCOURAGEMENT DEFIED

Joseph demonstrates that the difficulties we face do not neces-sarily demand that we yield to discouragement and defeat. Though I am sure Joseph wrestled with doubt and even depression, his dis-couraging moments were never debilitating. How easy it would have been for his discouragement to initiate moral failure. How convenient it would have been to blame God and go to bed with Potiphar's wife. How natural it would have been to get even with his brothers for what they had done.

Yet Joseph stood above it all. The concluding chapters of Genesis explain why Joseph was able to resist discouragement. We see that he had confidence in both the *presence* and *purpose* of God.

The phrase "The Lord was with Joseph" is repeated at critical stages—first when Joseph was in Potiphar's house and later after he had been sent to prison (Genesis 39:2, 21, 23). Joseph had an awareness of God's presence. When seduced by Potiphar's wife, Joseph didn't make some lame excuse. He was outspoken about his moral purity. He told her, "With me in charge, my master does not concern himself with anything in the house; everything he owns he has entrusted to my care. No one is greater in this house than I am. My master has withheld nothing from me except you, because you are his wife. How then could I do such a wicked thing and sin against God?" (vv. 8–9).

Because he was aware of God's presence, Joseph could not commit this wicked sin against God. Note too that he recognized his responsibility to his earthly master. This two-phased commit-ment is the strength of moral purity. People who are morally pure have an unflinching commitment to God and a sense of responsibil-ity to others. I don't know of any kind of moral failure that does not have an impact on our relationship with God or with others. When we sin sexually, we always violate relationships.

I am reminded of Christ's words, " 'Love the Lord your God with all your heart and with all your soul and with all your mind.' This is the first and greatest commandment. And the second is like it: 'Love your neighbor as yourself' " (Matthew 22:37–39). Love for God and love for others will drive us to purity.

Joseph's awareness of God's presence gave him the assurance of being able to carry on. It's not unlike God's encouragement to Joshua, "Have I not commanded you? Be strong and courageous. Do not be terrified; do not be discouraged, for the Lord your God will be with you wherever you go" (Joshua 1:9).

Righteousness might displace us in many ways, but it never displaces us from the presence of God. In fact, His presence is often felt more keenly and expressed with more conviction during displacement experiences. The hymn writer had it right when he wrote, "If Jesus goes with me, I'll go anywhere." It is our task—and our privilege—to trust in His presence (Psalm 139:7–12).

It is not until the end of Joseph's story that the second key to defying discouragement is revealed: the *purpose* of God. Take a close look at what Joseph said in his concluding remarks to his brothers: "Don't be afraid. Am I in the place of God? You intended to harm me, but God intended it for good to accomplish what is now being done, the saving of many lives" (Genesis 50:19–20). Joseph was convinced that God had a purpose in his difficulties. God had taken a confusing, unfair, and unjust chain of events and worked them together for His glory (Romans 8:28). Therefore, Joseph could forgive his brothers and get on with his life.

God's purpose in displacing Joseph from Canaan into Egypt was to place him where he could save the Messiah seed from starvation. There was only one righteous brother at the time who could be trusted with such an assignment. Joseph proved faithful.

God's purpose for Joseph in prison may have been twofold. To begin with, Joseph had a problem with arrogance. As a teenager he had bragged about his dreams and flaunted his coat of many colors, the badge of his father's favor, in front of his brothers. Three years in prison would knock him off his arrogant pedestal and tenderize Joseph's spirit so that his power would be exercised tenderly with his brothers. In prison he had a lot of time to think and to sort out who he was and should be. Prison for him was a time of refinement, a necessary process.

It is also possible that in this political prison Joseph met people who later were used by God to help him in his rise to government authority. God's purposes are sure, though not always seen. As we commit ourselves to righteousness, having an unflinching trust in a purposeful God will help counteract the power of discouragement.

Joseph's trust in God as a God of purpose was also the key to forgiveness. The brothers had no idea that their evil behavior had been used to advance God's cause. But Joseph came to realize that God is able to use even offensive and intentionally evil acts to accomplish His purpose. Why would Joseph seek revenge or maintain animosity toward tools that God used to bring about good? With this awareness, he was free to forgive his brothers.

When Jesus said, "Father, forgive them, for they do not know what they are doing" (Luke 23:34), He recognized that behind those wicked hands was the hand of God, accomplishing the most glorious event in history (Acts 2:23–24).

Walking in righteousness keeps us alert to the fact that God is at work in everything, even the things we tend to find offensive. This then enables us to forgive those who hurt and offend us. God will deal with those people. In the meantime, He will use their negative actions to produce His best through us.

The Conflict in Perspective

After seeing Joseph's determined commitment to righteousness, no matter what happened to him, we might expect him to be the inheritor of the messianic promise. But God's plan was different. While Satan was attempting to displace and disinherit Joseph, impacting him with a phenomenal sexual assault and the discouragement of imprisonment, God was extending the line of the Messiah through Joseph's brother, Judah. In God's sovereign theocratic control of the conflict, He was taking Satan's finest efforts and confounding them to His glory.

Yet as the book of Genesis concludes, God's sovereign victory is etched through Joseph's life. It was Joseph's perseverance for God that prevented Judah (and all the other brothers) from starving to death.

I'm reminded of God's response to Satan's best efforts, recorded by the psalmist: "Why do the nations conspire and the peoples plot in vain? The kings of the earth take their stand and the rulers gather together against the Lord and against his Anointed One. 'Let us break their chains,' they say, 'and throw off their fetters.' The One enthroned in heaven laughs; the Lord scoffs at them" (Psalm 2:1–4).

When I was a boy I learned a chorus that has more meaning now that I know of Joseph's victorious response to difficulty, induced by righteousness:

> Are we downhearted?
> No, no, no!
> Are we downhearted?
> No, no, no!
> Troubles may come and
> Troubles may go;
> We trust in Jesus
> Come weal or woe.
> Are we downhearted?
> No, no, no.

More significantly I find strength in Paul's words:

What, then, shall we say in response to this? If God is for us, who can be against us? He who did not spare his own Son, but gave him up for us all—how will he not also, along with him, graciously give us all things? Who will bring any charge against those whom God has chosen? It is God who justifies. Who is he that condemns? Christ Jesus, who died—more than that, who was raised to life—is at the right hand of God and is also interceding for us. Who shall separate us from the love of Christ? Shall trouble or hardship or persecution or famine or nakedness or danger or sword? As it is written: "For your sake we face death all day long; we are considered as sheep to be slaughtered." No, in all these things we are more than conquerors through him who loved us. For I am convinced that neither death nor life, neither angels nor demons, neither the present nor the future, nor any powers, nor height nor depth, nor anything else in all creation, will be able to separate us from the love of God that is in Christ Jesus our Lord. (Romans 8:31–39)

We have this treasure in jars of clay to show that this all-surpassing power is from God and not from us. We are hard pressed on every side, but not crushed; perplexed, but not in despair; persecuted, but not abandoned; struck down, but not destroyed. We always carry around in our body the death of Jesus, so that the life of Jesus may also be revealed in our body. For we who are alive are always being given over to death for Jesus' sake, so that his life may be revealed in our mortal body. (2 Corinthians 4:7–11)

Throughout the conflict in Genesis the upper stage of God's theocratic victory has preserved the promise of the kingdom of Christ. Though often threatened on the lower level by the careless-ness of God's people, Joseph closes this segment in biblical history by faithfully persevering. He won the victory through an unshaken confidence in the presence and purpose of God. We cheer him on. He is a true kingdom hero.

This issue that remains is whether I will help carry the victory for Christ and His kingdom. Will I someday hear, "Well done, good and faithful servant" (Matthew 25:21)? Or will I be an obstruction to the Messiah message by succumbing to the domain of the prince of this world?

Joshua laid out the options thousands of years ago, and the challenge remains for us: "Choose for yourselves this day whom you will serve. . . . As for me and my household, we will serve the Lord" (Joshua 24:15).

Questions for Your Personal Conflict

1. What situations or circumstances tend to cause you to become discouraged?

2. What is the situation you currently face which causes you the greatest sense of discouragement? How does it compare to Joseph's experiences in slavery and prison? What can you learn from Joseph to get beyond your feelings of discouragement?

3. Suppose a friend says, "I think people who are always discouraged *choose* to feel that way." How would you respond?

4. Read 1 Thessalonians 5:12–22. In a world where we're surrounded by discouragement, what are some ways we can become good *encouragers*?

5. As you reflect back on this book, what are the top three things you want to remember as you march forward to take your part in the kingdom conflict?

AFTERWORD

War. Battles. Conflict. Strategy.
These may be concepts that make us uncomfortable. We prefer lives that are smooth, peaceful, and tension free. Yet the kingdom conflict is both biblical and relevant to our lives today. Just because we don't enjoy discussing battle plans doesn't mean the war isn't taking place.

By this point, you should have an idea of specific strategies to watch out for. We should learn from the victories of those who have gone before us. And more importantly, we should learn from their mistakes. Why else would Scripture be so starkly honest about so many people's failures if not to teach us and give us the opportunity to avoid making the same blunders?

Above all, by now you should see that although things occasionally *appear* grim for those who follow God, nothing can ever prevent our eternal victory. With our futures secure, we are left with the challenge of making the most of our lives here and now. To a great extent, we determine the quality of our lives, based on the thoughts, words, and decisions of each day. The sooner we discover the responsibility (and the privilege) of suiting up in holy armor and standing firm in the kingdom conflict, the sooner our lives will take on exciting new meanings.

Although you've just completed this book, you're really just beginning. We took a cursory look at Genesis as we went along, but Genesis is only the first of sixty-six books of Scripture. If you keep reading (and I hope you will), you will find the kingdom conflict in every book. And if you read tomorrow's newspaper, you're likely to find numerous references there as well.

To be quite honest, all a book like this can do is try to *prepare* you for the conflict. Your degree of involvement, as always, is up to you. Experience will quickly teach you that life is never quite as safe on the front lines as it is when you try to keep the battle at a distance. But life is never as thrilling as it ought to be until you take your place on the front.

If you've been A.W.O.L. for a while, isn't it time to report for duty? The kingdom conflict continues. We need you.

Moody Press, a ministry of Moody Bible Institute,
is designed for education, evangelization, and edification.
If we may assist you in knowing more about Christ
and the Christian life, please write us without obligation:
Moody Press, c/o MLM, Chicago, Illinois 60610.